Selected Poems

Karl Shapiro
Selected Poems

Vintage Books

A Division of Random House / New York

Copyright 1940, 1941, 1942, 1943, 1944, 1945, 1946, 1947, 1948, 1949, 1950, 1951, 1952, 1953, 1954, © 1956, 1957, 1958, 1961, 1962, 1963, 1964, 1967, 1968 by Karl Shapiro.
Copyright renewed 1968, 1969, 1970, 1971, 1972, 1973 by Karl Shapiro.

All rights reserved under International and Pan-American Copyright Conventions. Published in the United States by Random House, Inc., New York, and simultaneously in Canada by Random House of Canada Limited, Toronto. Originally published by Random House, Inc., in April 1968.

Of the poems in this collection, 22 appeared originally in *The New Yorker*. Other poems have appeared in *Poetry* and *The Hudson Review*.

Library of Congress Cataloging in Publication Data
Shapiro, Karl Jay, 1913–
    Selected poems.
[PS3537.H27A6   1973]   811'.5'2   72–7402
ISBN 0–394–71875–5

COVER PHOTO: ROD JEW

Manufactured in the United States of America

First Vintage Books Edition, February 1973

FOR Teri

Contents

from V-Letter and Other Poems

from Person, Place and Thing

The Dome of Sunday

With focus sharp as Flemish-painted face
In film of varnish brightly fixed
And through a polished hand-lens deeply seen,
Sunday at noon through hyaline thin air
Sees down the street,
And in the camera of my eye depicts
Row-houses and row-lives:
Glass after glass, door after door the same,
Face after face the same, the same,
The brutal visibility the same;

As if one life emerging from one house
Would pause, a single image caught between
Two facing mirrors where vision multiplies
Beyond perspective,
A silent clatter in the high-speed eye
Spinning out photo-circulars of sight.

I see slip to the curb the long machines
Out of whose warm and windowed rooms pirouette
Shellacked with silk and light
The hard legs of our women.
Our women are one woman, dressed in black.
The carmine printed mouth
And cheeks as soft as muslin-glass belong
Outright to one dark dressy man,
Merely a swagger at her curvy side.
This is their visit to themselves:
All day from porch to porch they weave
A nonsense pattern through the even glare,
Stealing in surfaces
Cold vulgar glances at themselves.

And high up in the heated room all day
I wait behind the plate glass pane for one,
Hot as a voyeur for a glimpse of one,
The vision to blot out this woman's sheen;
All day my sight records expensively
Row-houses and row-lives.

But nothing happens; no diagonal
With melting shadow falls across the curb:
Neither the blinded negress lurching through fatigue,
Nor exiles bleeding from their pores,
Nor that bright bomb slipped lightly from its rack
To splinter every silvered glass and crystal prism,
Witch-bowl and perfume bottle
And billion candle-power dressing-bulb,
No direct hit to smash the shatter-proof
And lodge at last the quivering needle
Clean in the eye of one who stands transfixed
In fascination of her brightness.

Drug Store

I do remember an apothecary,
And hereabouts 'a dwells

It baffles the foreigner like an idiom,
And he is right to adopt it as a form
Less serious than the living-room or bar;
      For it disestablishes the café,
Is a collective, and on basic country.

Not that it praises hygiene and corrupts
The ice-cream parlor and the tobacconist's
Is it a center; but that the attractive symbols
      Watch over puberty and leer
Like rubber bottles waiting for sick-use.

Youth comes to jingle nickels and crack wise;
The baseball scores are his, the magazines
Devoted to lust, the jazz, the Coca-Cola,
      The lending-library of love's latest.
He is the customer; he is heroized.

And every nook and cranny of the flesh
Is spoken to by packages with wiles.
"Buy me, buy me," they whimper and cajole;
      The hectic range of lipsticks pouts,
Revealing the wicked and the simple mouth.

With scarcely any evasion in their eye
They smoke, undress their girls, exact a stance;
But only for a moment. The clock goes round;
      Crude fellowships are made and lost;
They slump in booths like rags, not even drunk.

The Fly

O hideous little bat, the size of snot,
With polyhedral eye and shabby clothes,
To populate the stinking cat you walk
The promontory of the dead man's nose,
Climb with the fine leg of a Duncan-Phyfe
   The smoking mountains of my food
      And in a comic mood
  In mid-air take to bed a wife.

Riding and riding with your filth of hair
On gluey foot or wing, forever coy,
Hot from the compost and green sweet decay,
Sounding your buzzer like an urchin toy—
You dot all whiteness with diminutive stool,
   In the tight belly of the dead
      Burrow with hungry head
  And inlay maggots like a jewel.

At your approach the great horse stomps and paws
Bringing the hurricane of his heavy tail;
Shod in disease you dare to kiss my hand
Which sweeps against you like an angry flail;
Still you return, return, trusting your wing
   To draw you from the hunter's reach
      That learns to kill to teach
  Disorder to the tinier thing.

My peace is your disaster. For your death
Children like spiders cup their pretty hands
And wives resort to chemistry of war.
In fens of sticky paper and quicksands
You glue yourself to death. Where you are stuck
   You struggle hideously and beg,
      You amputate your leg
  Imbedded in the amber muck.

But I, a man, must swat you with my hate,
Slap you across the air and crush your flight,
Must mangle with my shoe and smear your blood,
Expose your little guts pasty and white,
Knock your head sidewise like a drunkard's hat,
   Pin your wings under like a crow's,
      Tear off your flimsy clothes
And beat you as one beats a rat.

Then like Gargantua I stride among
The corpses strewn like raisins in the dust,
The broken bodies of the narrow dead
That catch the throat with fingers of disgust.
I sweep. One gyrates like a top and falls
   And stunned, stone blind, and deaf
      Buzzes its frightful F
And dies between three cannibals.

University

To hurt the Negro and avoid the Jew
Is the curriculum. In mid-September
The entering boys, identified by hats,
Wander in a maze of mannered brick
    Where boxwood and magnolia brood
    And columns with imperious stance
    Like rows of ante-bellum girls
       Eye them, outlanders.

In whited cells, on lawns equipped for peace,
Under the arch, and lofty banister,
Equals shake hands, unequals blankly pass;
The exemplary weather whispers, "Quiet, quiet"
    And visitors on tiptoe leave
    For the raw North, the unfinished West,
    As the young, detecting an advantage,
       Practice a face.

Where, on their separate hill, the colleges,
Like manor houses of an older law,
Gaze down embankments on a land in fee,
The Deans, dry spinsters over family plate,
    Ring out the English name like coin,
    Humor the snob and lure the lout.
    Within the precincts of this world
       Poise is a club.

But on the neighboring range, misty and high,
The past is absolute: some luckless race
Dull with inbreeding and conformity
Wears out its heart, and comes barefoot and bad
    For charity or jail. The scholar
    Sanctions their obsolete disease;
    The gentleman revolts with shame
       At his ancestor.

And the true nobleman, once a democrat,
Sleeps on his private mountain. He was one
Whose thought was shapely and whose dream was broad;
This school he held his art and epitaph.
    But now it takes from him his name,
    Falls open like a dishonest look,
    And shows us, rotted and endowed,
      Its senile pleasure.

Waitress

Whoever with the compasses of his eyes
Is plotting the voyage of your steady shape
As you come laden through the room and back
And rounding your even bottom like a Cape
Crooks his first finger, whistles through his lip
Till you arrive, all motion, like a ship,

He is my friend—consider his dark pangs
And love of Niger, naked indigence,
Dance him the menu of a poem and squirm
Deep in the juke-box jungle, green and dense.
Surely he files his teeth, punctures his nose,
Carves out the god and takes off all his clothes.

For once, the token on the table's edge
Sufficing, proudly and with hair unpinned
You mounted the blueplate, stretched out and grinned
Like Christmas fish and turkey pink and skinned,
Eyes on the half-shell, loin with parsley stuck,
Thigh-bones and ribs and little toes to suck.

I speak to you, ports of the northern myth,
This dame is carved and eaten. One by one,
God knows what hour, her different parts go home,
Lastly her pants, and day or night is done;
But on the restaurant the sign of fear
Reddens and blazes—"English spoken here."

Mongolian Idiot

A dog that spoke, a monster born of sheep
We mercilessly kill, and kill the thought,
Yet house the parrot and let the centaur go,
These being to their nature and those not.
We laugh at apes, that never quite succeed
       At eating soup or wearing hats.

Adam had named so many but not this,
This that would name a curse when it had come,
Unfinished man, or witch, or myth, or sin,
Not ever father and never quite a son.
Ape had outstripped him, dog and darling lamb
       And all the kindergarten beasts.

Enter the bare room of his mind and count
His store of words with letters large and black;
See how he handles clumsily those blocks
With swans and sums; his colored picture books.
At thirty-five he squeals to see the ball
       Bounce in the air and roll away.

Pity and fear we give this innocent
Who maimed his mother's beautiful instinct;
But she would say, "My body had a dog;
I bore the ape and nursed the crying sheep.
He is my kindness and my splendid gift
       Come from all life and for all life."

Israfel

la tombe de Poe éblouissante

Picture the grave in his diabolical dream
Where death would come with clues and scenery,
The bulbous forehead and the crooked mouth
Leaking a poison, the translucent hands.

Perhaps like Juliet he could come alive
To hate Longfellow and to outrage life,
But dare not from his wretched rusty stone,
Landmark for girls developing in slums.

Here he is local color, another crank;
Pawnshops and whores and sour little bars
Accept him. Neither alarming nor prophetic,
He pleases like a wop or a jack-o-lantern.

Others uptown forgive his nasty eyes
Because he was sick and had a mind to err;
But he was never dirty like Hawthorne,
But boyish with his spooks and funerals

And clammy virgins. What else were his codes
But diagrams of hideouts of the mind
Plugged up with corpses and expensive junk,
Prosopopoeia to keep himself at bay?

Think of him as a cicerone with data
False as a waxworks and that understood
Ask pitifully for pain. Or think that now
Four cities claim him as France recommended.

Hospital

Inside or out, the key is pain. It holds
The florist to your pink medicinal rose,
The nickname to the corpse. One wipes it from
Blue German blades or drops it down the drain;
The novelist with a red tube up his nose
Gingerly pets it. Nurse can turn it off.

This is the Oxford of all sicknesses.
Kings have lain here and fabulous small Jews
And actresses whose legs were always news.
In this black room the painter lost his sight,
The crippled dancer here put down her shoes,
And the scholar's memory broke, like an old clock.

These reached to heaven and inclined their heads
While starchy angels reached them into beds:
These stooped to hell to labor out their time,
Or choked to death in seas of glaucous slime:
All tasted fire, and then, their hate annealed,
Ate sad ice-cream and wept upon a child.

What church is this, what factory of souls
Makes the bad good and fashions a new nose,
And the doctors reel with Latin and even the dead
Expect the unexpected? For O the souls
Fly back like heavy homing-birds to roost
In long-racked limbs, filling the lonely boughs.

The dead cry *life* and stagger up the hill;
But is there still the incorrigible city where
The well enjoy their poverty and the young
Worship the gutter? Is Wednesday still alive
And Tuesday wanting terribly to sin?
Hush, there are many pressing the oak doors,

Saying, "Are boys and girls important fears?
Can you predict the elections by my guts?"
But the rubber gloves are deep in a deep wound,
Stitching a single heart. These far surpass
Themselves, their wives, and the removed goitre;
Are, for the most part, human but unbandaged.

Haircut

O wonderful nonsense of lotions of Lucky Tiger,
Of savory soaps and oils of bottle-bright green,
The gold of liqueurs, the unguents of Newark and Niger,
Powders and balms and waters washing me clean;

In mirrors of marble and silver I see us forever
Increasing, decreasing the puzzles of luminous spaces
As I turn, am revolved and am pumped in the air on a lever,
With the backs of my heads in chorus with all of my faces.

Scissors and comb are mowing my hair into neatness,
Now pruning my ears, now smoothing my neck like a plain;
In the harvest of hair and the chaff of powdery sweetness
My snow-covered slopes grow dark with the wooly rain.

And the little boy cries, for it hurts to sever the curl,
And we too are quietly bleating to part with our coat.
Does the barber want blood in a dish? I am weak as a girl,
I desire my pendants, the fatherly chin of a goat.

I desire the pants of a bear, the nap of a monkey
Which trousers of friction have blighted down to my skin.
I am bare as a tusk, as jacketed up as a flunkey,
With the chest of a moth-eaten camel growing within.

But in death we shall flourish, you summer-dark leaves of my
        head,
While the flesh of the jaw ebbs away from the shores of my
        teeth;
You shall cover my sockets and soften the boards of my bed
And lie on the flat of my temples as proud as a wreath.

A Cut Flower

I stand on slenderness all fresh and fair,
I feel root-firmness in the earth far down,
I catch in the wind and loose my scent for bees
That sack my throat for kisses and suck love.
What is the wind that brings thy body over?
Wind, I am beautiful and sick. I long
For rain that strikes and bites like cold and hurts.
Be angry, rain, for dew is kind to me
When I am cool from sleep and take my bath.

Who softens the sweet earth about my feet,
Touches my face so often and brings water?
Where does she go, taller than any sunflower
Over the grass like birds? Has she a root?
These are great animals that kneel to us,
Sent by the sun perhaps to help us grow.
I have seen death. The colors went away,
The petals grasped at nothing and curled tight.
Then the whole head fell off and left the sky.

She tended me and held me by my stalk.
Yesterday I was well, and then the gleam,
The thing sharper than frost cut me in half.
I fainted and was lifted high. I feel
Waist-deep in rain. My face is dry and drawn.
My beauty leaks into the glass like rain.
When first I opened to the sun I thought
My colors would be parched. Where are my bees?
Must I die now? Is this a part of life?

Auto Wreck

Its quick soft silver bell beating, beating,
And down the dark one ruby flare
Pulsing out red light like an artery,
The ambulance at top speed floating down
Past beacons and illuminated clocks
Wings in a heavy curve, dips down,
And brakes speed, entering the crowd.
The doors leap open, emptying light;
Stretchers are laid out, the mangled lifted
And stowed into the little hospital.
Then the bell, breaking the hush, tolls once,
And the ambulance with its terrible cargo
Rocking, slightly rocking, moves away,
As the doors, an afterthought, are closed.

We are deranged, walking among the cops
Who sweep glass and are large and composed.
One is still making notes under the light.
One with a bucket douches ponds of blood
Into the street and gutter.
One hangs lanterns on the wrecks that cling,
Empty husks of locusts, to iron poles.

Our throats were tight as tourniquets,
Our feet were bound with splints, but now,
Like convalescents intimate and gauche,
We speak through sickly smiles and warn
With the stubborn saw of common sense,
The grim joke and the banal resolution.
The traffic moves around with care,
But we remain, touching a wound
That opens to our richest horror.
Already old, the question Who shall die?
Becomes unspoken Who is innocent?

For death in war is done by hands;
Suicide has cause and stillbirth, logic;
And cancer, simple as a flower, blooms.
But this invites the occult mind,
Cancels our physics with a sneer,
And spatters all we knew of denouement
Across the expedient and wicked stones.

Scyros

The doctor punched my vein
The captain called me Cain
Upon my belly sat the sow of fear
With coins on either eye
The President came by
And whispered to the braid what none could hear

High over where the storm
Stood steadfast cruciform
The golden eagle sank in wounded wheels
White Negroes laughing still
Crept fiercely on Brazil
Turning the navies upward on their keels

Now one by one the trees
Stripped to their naked knees
To dance upon the heaps of shrunken dead
The roof of England fell
Great Paris tolled her bell
And China staunched her milk and wept for bread

No island singly lay
But lost its name that day
The Ainu dived across the plunging sands
From dawn to dawn to dawn
King George's birds came on
Strafing the tulips from his children's hands

Thus in the classic sea
Southeast from Thessaly
The dynamited mermen washed ashore
And tritons dressed in steel
Trolled heads with rod and reel
And dredged potatoes from the Aegean floor

Hot is the sky and green
Where Germans have been seen
The moon leaks metal on the Atlantic fields
Pink boys in birthday shrouds
Loop lightly through the clouds
Or coast the peaks of Finland on their shields

That prophet year by year
Lay still but could not hear
Where scholars tapped to find his new remains
Gog and Magog ate pork
In vertical New York
And war began next Wednesday on the Danes

Buick

As a sloop with a sweep of immaculate wing on her delicate
  spine
And a keel as steel as a root that holds in the sea as she leans,
Leaning and laughing, my warm-hearted beauty, you ride, you
  ride,
You tack on the curves with parabola speed and a kiss of
  goodbye,
Like a thoroughbred sloop, my new high-spirited spirit, my
  kiss.

As my foot suggests that you leap in the air with your hips
  of a girl,
My finger that praises your wheel and announces your voices
  of song,
Flouncing your skirts, you blueness of joy, you flirt of politeness,
You leap, you intelligence, essence of wheelness with silvery
  nose,
And your platinum clocks of excitement stir like the hairs of a
  fern.

But how alien you are from the booming belts of your birth
  and the smoke
Where you turned on the stinging lathes of Detroit and Lan-
  sing at night
And shrieked at the torch in your secret parts and the amorous
  tests,
But now with your eyes that enter the future of roads you
  forget;
You are all instinct with your phosphorous glow and your
  streaking hair.

And now when we stop it is not as the bird from the shell that
    I leave
Or the leathery pilot who steps from his bird with a sneer of
    delight,
And not as the ignorant beast do you squat and watch me
    depart,
But with exquisite breathing you smile, with satisfaction of
    love,
And I touch you again as you tick in the silence and settle in
    sleep.

Giantess

When Nature once in lustful hot undress
Conceived gargantuan offspring, then would I
Have loved to live near a young giantess,
Like a voluptuous cat at a queen's feet.

To see her body flower with her desire
And freely spread out in its dreadful play,
Guess if her heart concealed some heavy fire
Whose humid smokes would swim upon her eye;

To feel at leisure her stupendous shapes,
Crawl on the cliffs of her enormous knees,
And, when the unhealthy summer suns fatigued,

Have her stretch out across the plains and so
Sleep in the shadows of her breasts at ease
Like a small hamlet at a mountain's base.

(Baudelaire translation)

Conscription Camp

Your landscape sickens with a dry disease
Even in May, Virginia, and your sweet pines
Like Frenchmen runted in a hundred wars
Are of a child's height in these battlefields.

For Wilson sowed his teeth where generals prayed
—High-sounding Lafayette and sick-eyed Lee—
The loud Elizabethan crashed your swamps
Like elephants and the subtle Indian fell.

Is it for love, you ancient-minded towns,
That on the tidy grass of your great graves
And on your roads and riverways serene
Between the corn with green flags in a row,

Wheat amorous as hair and hills like breasts
Each generation, ignorant of the last,
Mumbling in sheds, embarrassed to salute,
Comes back to choke on etiquette of hate?

You manufacture history like jute—
Labor is cheap, Virginia, for high deeds,
But in your British dream of reputation
The black man is your conscience and your cost.

Here on the plains perfect for civil war
The clapboard city like a weak mirage
Of order rises from the sand to house
These thousands and the paranoid Monroe;

The sunrise gun rasps in the throat of heaven;
The lungs of dawn are heavy and corrupt;
We hawk and spit; our flag walks through the air
Breathing hysteria thickly in each face.

Through the long school of day, absent in heart,
Distant in every thought but self we tread,
Wheeling in blocks like large expensive toys
That never understand except through fun.

To steal aside as aimlessly as curs
Is our desire; to stare at corporals
As sceptically as boys; not to believe
The misty-eyed letter and the cheap snapshot.

To cross the unnatural frontier of your name
Is our free dream, Virginia, and beyond,
White and unpatriotic in our beds,
To rise from sleep like driftwood out of surf.

But stricter than parole is this same wall
And these green clothes, a secret on the fields,
In towns betray us to the arresting touch
Of lady-wardens, good and evil wives.

And far and fabulous is the word "Outside"
Like "Europe" when the midnight liners sailed,
Leaving a wake of ermine on the tide
Where rubies drowned and eyes were softly drunk.

Still we abhor your news and every voice
Except the Personal Enemy's, and songs
That pumped by the great central heart of love
On tides of energy at evening come.

Instinctively to break your compact law
Box within box, Virginia, and throw down
The dangerous bright habits of pure form
We struggle hideously and cry for fear.

And like a very tired whore who stands
Wrapped in the sensual crimson of her art
High in the tired doorway of a street
And beckons half-concealed the passerby,

The sun, Virginia, on your Western stairs
Pauses and smiles away between the trees,
Motioning the soldier overhill to town
To his determined hungry burst of joy.

Washington Cathedral

From summer and the wheel-shaped city
That sweats like a swamp and wrangles on
Its melting streets, white mammoth Forums,
And political hotels with awnings, caryatids;
Past barricaded embassies with trees
That shed trash and parch his eyes,
To here, the acres of superior quiet,
Shadow and damp, the tourist comes,
And, cooled by stones and darkness, stares.

Tall as a lover's night, the nave
Broods over him, irradiates,
And stars of color out of painted glass
Shoot downward on apostles and on chairs
Huddled by hundreds under altar rails.
Yet it is only Thursday; there are no prayers,

But exclamations. The lady invokes by name
The thousand-odd small sculptures, spooks,
New angels, pitted roods; she gives
The inventory of relics to his heart
That aches with history and astonishment:
He gives a large coin to a wooden coffer.

Outside, noon blazes in his face like guns.
He goes down by the Bishop's walk, the dial,
The expensive grass, the Byzantine bench,
While stark behind him a red naked crane
Hangs over the unfinished transept,
A Cubist hen rivalling the Gothic School.

Whether he sees the joke; whether he cares;
Whether he tempts a vulgar miracle,
Some deus ex machina, this is his choice,
A shrine of whispers and tricky penumbras.

      Therefore he votes again for the paid
Clergy, the English hint, the bones of Wilson
Crushed under tons of fake magnificence.

        Nor from the zoo of his instincts
        Come better than crude eagles: now
He cannot doubt that violent obelisk
And Lincoln whittled to a fool's colossus.
This church and city triumph in his eyes.
He is only a good alien, nominally happy.

The Twins

Likeness has made them animal and shy.
See how they turn their full gaze left and right,
Seeking the other, yet not moving close;
Nothing in their relationship is gross,
But soft, conspicuous, like giraffes. And why
Do they not speak except by sudden sight?

Sisters kiss freely and unsubtle friends
Wrestle like lovers; brothers loudly laugh:
These in a dreamier bondage dare not touch.
Each is the other's soul and hears too much
The heartbeat of the other; each apprehends
The sad duality and the imperfect half.

The one lay sick, the other wandered free,
But like a child to a small plot confined
Walked a short way and dumbly reappeared.
Is it not all-in-all of what they feared,
The single death, the obvious destiny
That maims the miracle their will designed?

For they go emptily from face to face,
Keeping the instinctive partnership of birth
A ponderous marriage and a sacred name;
Theirs is the pride of shouldering each the same
The old indignity of Esau's race
And Dromio's denouement of tragic mirth.

Travelogue for Exiles

Look and remember. Look upon this sky;
Look deep and deep into the sea-clean air,
The unconfined, the terminus of prayer.
Speak now and speak into the hallowed dome.
What do you hear? What does the sky reply?
The heavens are taken: this is not your home.

Look and remember. Look upon this sea;
Look down and down into the tireless tide.
What of a life below, a life inside,
A tomb, a cradle in the curly foam?
The waves arise; sea-wind and sea agree
The waters are taken: this is not your home.

Look and remember. Look upon this land,
Far, far across the factories and the grass.
Surely, there, surely, they will let you pass.
Speak then and ask the forest and the loam.
What do you hear? What does the land command?
The earth is taken: this is not your home.

Terminal

Over us stands the broad electric face
With semaphores that flick into the gaps,
Notching the time on sixtieths of space,
Springing the traveller through the folded traps
Downstairs with luggage anywhere to go
While others happily toil upward too;
Well-dressed or stricken, banished or restored,
Hundreds step down and thousands get aboard.

In neat confusion, tickets in our brain
We press the hard plush to our backs and sigh;
The brakeman thumbs his watch, the children strain
The windows to their smeary sight—Goodbye,
The great car creaks, the stone wall turns away
And lights flare past like fishes undersea;
Heads rolling heavily and all as one
With languid screams we charge into the sun.

Now through the maelstrom of the town we ride
Clicking with speed like skates on solid ice;
Streets drop and buildings silently collide,
Rails spread apart, converge and neatly splice.
Through gasping blanks of air we pound and ford
Bulking our courage forward like a road,
Climbing the world on long dead-level stairs
With catwalk stilts and trestles hung by hairs.

Out where the oaks on wide turntables grow
And constellation hamlets gyre and glow,
The straight-up bridges dive and from below
The river's sweet eccentric borders flow;
Into the culverts sliced like lands of meat,
Armies of cornstalks on their ragged feet,
And upward-outward toward the blueback hill
Where clouds of thunder graze and drink their fill.

And always at our side, swifter than we
The racing rabbits of the wire lope
And in their blood the words at liberty
Outspeed themselves; but on our rail we grope
Drinking from one white wire overhead
Hot drinks of action and hell's fiery feed.
Lightly the finger-shaped antennae feel
And lightly cheer the madness of our wheel.

We turn, we turn, thrumming the harp of sounds
And all is pleasure's move, motion of joy;
Now we imagine that we go like hounds
And now like sleds and now like many a toy
Coming alive on Christmas Day to crawl
Between the great world of the floor and wall,
But on the peak of speed we flag and fall—
Fixed on the air we do not move at all.

Arrived at space we settle in our car
And stare like souls admitted to the sky;
Nothing at length is close at hand or far;
All feats of image vanish from the eye.
Upon our brow is set the bursting star,
Upon the void the wheel and axle-bar,
The planetary fragments broken lie;
Distance is dead and light can only die.

The Snob

At what time in its little history
Did on the matrix of his brain a blow
Fall that struck like a relentless die
And left him speechless; or was it by degrees
That the algid folds of mind, caught in a pose,
            Hardened and set like concrete,
Printing and fixing a distorted moment?

Nothing but death will smash this ugly cast
That wears its trade mark big upon its face,
A scutcheon for Greek-letter brotherhoods
Where it is weakly sworn by smiles to cow
Unequals, niggers or just Methodists.
            His bearing is a school of thought,
But he is not funny and not unimportant.

A Robbery

By day I had dispraised their life,
Accused foremost the little cheated wives
Whose hands like trailers ludicrously hitched
To husbands, over the graph of business bump.
As often, with my friend, I laughed at them,
All but their young, whose strenuous anarchy
        Asked Why and promised war.

So of their legal dark of nights,
And bed revenge, and competent small births
That shut us out from marriage, I despaired:
Men brought home hate like evening papers, maids
Longed for their slums, the inarticulate clock
Spoke once, and faces, double-locked and still,
        Turned to the wall to sleep.

I show that fear unearthed that Boy.
Into the taut membrane of night, like knives
A woman screams, rending with rape our rest.
Bodies are ripped from beds; the snapped dream hangs:
And quick to plunge the torn portieres of sleep
We race soft-running Horror the length of halls.
        Ghouls are at every door.

Down in the hostile dark, as one,
The heavy faces point, close in, take aim,
And hands describe centripetal broad Wheels
Through which unseen a wiry robber moves.
Voices enlarge, cops clamber from the sky,
Our sudden symmetry dissolves. We laugh.
        "Nothing is caught, or lost."

Yet our emergency is lost,
Which would have, naked in the domestic night,
Brought us like actual murder to relief.
Boys have mixed blood and kissed to seal an oath.
Boys have an oath. O we were close to boys,
The salesman, the real estator, the clerk, and I,
Their enemy, their poet.

Robber, paid agent of our hate,
I kiss my hand to you across the roofs
And jungle of back alleys where you hide.
You with your guns are like a boy I loved.
He was born dead and never had a name.
He was my little son. Night took him off.
Hard to unlearn is love.

October 1

That season when the leaf deserts the bole
And half-dead see-saws through the October air
Falling face-downward on the walks to print
The decalcomania of its little soul—
Hardly has the milkman's sleepy horse
On wooden shoes echoed across the blocks,
When with its back jaws open like a dredge
The van comes lumbering up the curb to someone's door and
      knocks.

And four black genii muscular and shy
Holding their shy caps enter the first room
Where someone hurriedly surrenders up
The thickset chair, the mirror half awry,
Then to their burdens stoop without a sound.
One with his bare hands rends apart the bed,
One stuffs the china-barrel with stale print,
Two bear the sofa toward the door with dark funereal tread.

The corner lamp, the safety eye of night,
Enveloped in the sun blinks and goes blind
And soon the early risers pick their way
Through kitchenware and pillows bolt upright.
The bureau on the sidewalk with bare back
And wrinkling veneer is most disgraced,
The sketch of Paris suffers in the wind,
Only the bike, its nose against the wall, does not show haste.

Two hours—the movers mop their necks and look,
Filing through dust and echoes back and forth.
The halls are hollow and all the floors are cleared
Bare to the last board, to the most secret nook;
But on the street a small chaos survives
That slowly now the leviathan ingests,
And schoolboys and stenographers stare at
The truck, the house, the husband in his hat who stands and
    rests.

He turns with miserable expectant face
And for the last time enters. On the wall
A picture-stain spreads from the nail-hole down.
Each object live and dead has left its trace.
He leaves his key; but as he quickly goes
This question comes behind: Did someone die?
Is someone rich or poor, better or worse?
What shall uproot a house and bring this care into his eye?

Necropolis

Even in death they prosper; even in the death
Where lust lies senseless and pride fallow
The mouldering owners of rents and labor
Prosper and improve the high hill.

For theirs is the stone whose name is deepest cut,
Theirs the facsimile temple, theirs
The iron acanthus and the hackneyed Latin,
The boxwood rows and all the birds.

And even in death the poor are thickly herded
In intimate congestion under streets and alleys.
Look at the standard sculpture, the cheap
Synonymous slabs, the machined crosses.

Yes, even in death the cities are unplanned.
The heirs govern from the old centers;
They will not remove. And the ludicrous angels,
Remains of the poor, will never fly
But only multiply in the green grass.

My Grandmother

My grandmother moves to my mind in context of sorrow
And, as if apprehensive of near death, in black;
Whether erect in chair, her dry and corded throat harangued
    by grief,
Or at ragged book bent in Hebrew prayer,
Or gentle, submissive, and in tears to strangers;
Whether in sunny parlor or back of drawn blinds.

Though time and tongue made any love disparate,
On daguerreotype with classic perspective
Beauty I sigh and soften at is hers.
I pity her life of deaths, the agony of her own,
But most that history moved her through
Stranger lands and many houses,
Taking her exile for granted, confusing
The tongues and tasks of her children's children.

Midnight Show

The year is done, the last act of the vaudeville,
The last top hat and patent leather tappity-tap
Enclosed in darkness. Pat. Blackout. Only the organ
Groans, groans, its thousand golden throats in love;
While blue lowlight suffuses mysteries of sleep
Through racks of heads, and smoothly parts the gauzy veil
That slips, the last pretense of peace, into the wings.

With a raucous crash the music rises to its feet,
And pouring from the hidden eye like God the Light
The light white-molten cold fills out the vacant field
With shattered cities, striped ships, and maps with lines
That crawl—symbols of horror, symbols of obscenity;
A girl astride a giant cannon, holding a flag;
Removal of stone and stained-glass saints from a known
        cathedral;

And the Voice, the loving and faithful pointer, trots beside
Reel after reel, taking death in its well-trained stride.
The Voice, the polite, the auctioneer, places his hints
Like easy bids. The lab assistant, the Voice, dips
Their pity like litmus papers into His rancid heart.—
Dream to be surfeited, nerves clogged up with messages,
And, backed up at the ganglion, the news refused.

Dream to be out in snow where every corner Santa,
Heart of one generation's dreams, tinkles a bell.
We know him too. He is the Unemployed, but clowns
As the Giver, receiving pennies in a cast-iron pot.
Dream to be cold with Byrd at the world's bottom. Dream
To be warm in the Vatican, photographing a manuscript.
Dream to be there, a cell in Europe's poisoned blood.

Revulsion cannot rouse our heads for pride or protest.
The eye sees as the camera, a clean moronic gaze,
And to go is not impossible but merely careless.
O wife, what shall we tell the children that we saw?
O son, what shall we tell our father? And O my friend,
What shall we tell our senses when the lights go up
And noiselessly the golden curtains crash together!

Honkytonk

Taken as diagram of Mind that marks,
Led by an arrow, green perimeters
Where thoughts sip peace and garden; inward then
To suffering junctions, slums kicked by a boot,
   Arpeggios of porches:
   Decision, Anger, Pride,
Like Self-Reproach the city points to this
Its maudlin slapping heart, our origin.

Then at the outskirts of our Conscious, No
From old high-over offices beats down
On standard faces Business-mad, and girls,
Grass under sullen stone, grown pale with work;
   Yet shields with shadow this
   Disgraced like genitals
Ghetto of local sin, laughable Hell,
Night's very alley, loathed but let alone.

I say to harass projects of decorum
This is maintained by kids, police, douceurs,
And ravenous for marvels, rancid Jews.
Callow as brass, their eyes on nipples snagged,
   Snagged in the jaded hair,
   Goaded by silken legs,
They mill around, bacterial and bright,
Seeking outbreaks of pain, their bitter milk.

Who needs Revenge or Fear can buy: in bars
Murals of lust, and talk; movies for men;
A waxworks of syphilitics; shooting range,
Phrenologist and tattoo artist; all
   Quacks who apprehend
   And speak the dirty word.
But oh, ridiculously lost those four
Hymning salvation at the Burlesk door.

How elemental ions of pure joy
Convert to deadly sins, and bump like trucks
Uptown to roads instinctive to the young,
I only ask. But in and out they go
        Satanic to discover
        Imago of Unrest
Whose Ultima Thule is a general low
And obscene civics of our self-distrust.

Hollywood

Farthest from any war, unique in time
Like Athens or Baghdad, this city lies
Between dry purple mountains and the sea.
The air is clear and famous, every day
Bright as a postcard, bringing bungalows
    And sights. The broad nights advertise
For love and music and astronomy.

Heart of a continent, the hearts converge
On open boulevards where palms are nursed
With flare-pots like a grove, on villa roads
Where castles cultivated like a style
Breed fabulous metaphors in foreign stone,
    And on enormous movie lots
Where history repeats its vivid blunders.

Alice and Cinderella are most real.
Here may the tourist, quite sincere at last,
Rest from his dream of travels. All is new,
No ruins claim his awe, and permanence,
Despised like customs, fails at every turn.
    Here where the eccentric thrives,
Laughter and love are leading industries.

Luck is another. Here the bodyguard,
The parasite, the scholar are well paid,
The quack erects his alabaster office,
The moron and the genius are enshrined,
And the mystic makes a fortune quietly;
    Here all superlatives come true
And beauty is marketed like a basic food.

O can we understand it? Is it ours,
A crude whim of a beginning people,
A private orgy in a secluded spot?
Or alien like the word *harem*, or true
Like hideous Pittsburgh or depraved Atlanta?
   Is adolescence just as vile
As this its architecture and its talk?

Or are they parvenus, like boys and girls?
Or ours and happy, cleverest of all?
Yes. Yes. Though glamorous to the ignorant
This is the simplest city, a new school.
What is more nearly ours? If soul can mean
   The civilization of the brain,
This is a soul, a possible proud Florence.

Guineapig

What do you care, dear total stranger,
For the successful failure of my safest danger,
My pig in the poke or dog in the manger,

Or who does what in the where of his chamber
Probing for his gallstones and the rods of amber
When the succubae sing and the accusers clamber?

Tooth for a Tooth, O why will you wander
After somebody's anybody's body to squander?
Do the heads grow bald as the hands grow fonder?

Thank you. Your kiss of conditional surrender
Reminds me of the case of dubious gender
Who died on the verge of gaining a defender.

Then read it and weep, dear lovelorn panther;
Change your pajamas and fill the decanter;
Down with the dreamwork and long live the banter.

The Glutton

The jowls of his belly crawl and swell like the sea
When his mandibles oily with lust champ and go wide;
Eternal, the springs of his spittle leak at the lips
Suspending the tongue like a whale that rolls on the tide.

His hands are as rotten fruit. His teeth are as corn.
Deep are the wells of his eyes and like navels, blind.
Dough is the brain that supplies his passion with bread.
Dough is the loose-slung sack of his great behind.

Will his paps become woman's? He dreams of the yielding of
      milk,
Despising the waste of his stool that recalls him to bread;
More than passion of sex and the transverse pains of disease
He thinks of starvation, the locked-up mouth of the dead.

I am glad that his stomach will eat him away in revenge,
Digesting itself when his blubber is lain in the earth.
Let the juice of his gluttony swallow him inward like lime
And leave of his volume only the mould of his girth.

Elegy For Two Banjos

Haul up the flag, you mourners,
　　　Not half-mast but all the way;
The funeral is done and disbanded;
　　　The devil's had the final say.

O mistress and wife too pensive,
　　　Pallbearers and priestly men,
Put your black clothes in the attic,
　　　And get up on your feet again.

Death did his job like a scholar,
　　　A most unusual case,
Death did his job like a gentleman;
　　　He barely disturbed the face.

You packed him in a handsome carton,
　　　Set the lid with silver screws;
You dug a dark pit in the graveyard
　　　To tell the white worms the news.

Now you've nothing left to remember,
　　　Nothing but the words he wrote,
But they'll never let you remember,
　　　Only stick like a bone in your throat.

O if I'd been his wife or mistress,
　　　His pallbearer or his parish priest,
I'd have kept him at home forever—
　　　Or as long as bric-a-brac at least.

I would have burned his body
　　　And salvaged a sizeable bone
For a paper-weight or a door-stop
　　　Or a garden flagstone.

I would have heaped the fire
      And boiled his beautiful skull.
It was laden like a ship for travels
      And now is but an empty hull.

I would have dried it off in linens,
      Polished it with a chamois cloth
Till it shone like a brand-new quarter
      And felt smooth as the nose of a moth.

Or I'd have hung it out in the garden
      Where everything else is alive,
Put a queen bee in the brain case
      So the bees could build a hive.

Maybe I'd have wired the jawbone
      With a silver spring beneath,
Set it in the cradle with baby
      So baby could rattle the teeth.

O you didn't do right by William
      To shove him down that filthy hole,
Throw him a lot of tears and Latin
      And a cheap "God bless your soul."

You might as well leave off mourning,
      His photograph is getting dim,
So you'd better take a long look at it
      For it's all you'll ever see of him.

Haul up the flag, you mourners,
      Not half-mast but all the way;
The funeral is done and disbanded;
      The devil's had the final say.

Epitaph for John and Richard

There goes the clock; there goes the sun;
Greenwich is right with Arlington;
The signal's minutes are signifying
That somebody old has finished dying,
That somebody young has just begun.

What do you think you earned today
Except the waste, except the pay,
Except the power to be spending?
And now your year is striking, ending,
What do you think you have put away?

Only a promise, only a life
Squandered in secret with a wife
In bedtime feigning and unfeigning;
The blood has long since ceased complaining;
The clock has satisfied the strife.

They will not cast your honored head
Or say from lecterns what you said,
But only keep you with them all
Committed in the City Hall;
Once born, once married, and once dead.

Emporium

He must have read Aladdin who rubbed his head
And brought this out of space; some genie came
With bolts of lawn and rugs of heavy red,
Shoes for white boxes, gems for velvet trays;
For who could authorize in his right name
Such pricelessness of time and recklessness of days?

Not Faust, who longed for Hell, would sell his light
For moving stairs and mirrors set in miles
Where wives might wander with their sex in sight;
Rage and rat's-logic this man must have known
Who built these buttresses on rotted piles,
Initialed every brick, and carved his lips in stone.

As if the ancient principle obtained
And solvent time would underwrite his debt,
Or the strong face of flesh were not profaned
For mannikins with hair of cloth-of-gold;
As if no tongue had ever questioned yet
Who buys and who is bought, who sells and who is sold.

But those politely dressed in normal drab
Shall think of him remotely, think with shame
How of their skill, their goodness and their gab
He trained his joys to be obsequious Jews;
At last not even wives shall goad his name
To feats of wealth, humility, and sickness-news;

So that, with rounded ruins honored, like Stonehenge,
Time shall have time, and he his impotent revenge.

Elegy Written on a Frontporch

The sun burns on its sultry wick;
Stratus and cumulus unite.
I who am neither well nor sick
Sit in a wicker chair and write.

A hot wind presses at my lips.
I peel. Am totally undressed.
Pinkish, as through a part-eclipse,
Heat licks upon my naked breast.

Angles in quick succession rise.
Eyesight is stereopticon
As roof and roof geometrize
Perspective deviously drawn.

I face a heaven half-destroyed,
A skyscape alabaster, dead.
One living shadow on the void,
A Flying Fortress drones ahead.

Motion and fixity take shape;
The fallow rays intensify
Distinctness. Nothing can escape
The clean hard focus of the eye.

Noise into humming noise constricts;
The traffic mumbles deeper down.
Only a trolley contradicts,
Ticks by neurotically to town.

Stretched taut upon the light I scorch,
Writhe in my sweat and smoke and sun.
The evening paper hits the porch;
My honeymoon of peace is done.

Unmasticated pulp of life . . .
Decision finds me blind and deaf.
I do not finger for the strife
Of Delano and Mutt and Jeff,

Or bend upon my nudity's
Umbilicus, the fact of facts,
As one who drowns in light and sees
The newsreel of his private acts.

I do not hug my feet with glee
And smile into my cul-de-sac
Enamoured of the dignity
Of facing forward moving back.

But set my wired sight, reclaim
The rotted friendship and the fresh;
Tune in on him who changed his name
And her who stultified the flesh.

I see who came to marriage raw
With poverty and self-abuse;
Defendants to the general law,
Their ignorance was no excuse.

Instructors, graduates I see,
Scholars who sneered into their books,
The female doctors pouring tea,
Hundreds of victims of their looks.

The money-poise of some, the pride
Of those who whored on easy checks,
Sons of The Business, dressy, snide,
Disfigured in expensive wrecks.

Believers in the songhit, thin
With pounding to the hebroid jazz;
The studious drinkers feeding in
The cloaca of the middle-class.

I see too many who romanced
Defeat, unmasculine, debased;
The striptease puritans who danced
The long lewd ritual of waste.

All these I bury out of sight
Sans benefit of epitaph.
I turn my legs into the light,
Punch out a cigarette and laugh.

For one, the best against that rout,
Deserted, obdurate to see
Their weakly literate wear out
The old Horatian fallacy;

Spoke of the beauty-to-obey,
The life-expectancy of bone.
She turned her back upon the day
But will not lie at night alone

Death of Emma Goldman

Triumphant at the final breath,
  Their senile God, their cops,
All the authorities and friends pro tem
Passing her pillow, keeping her concerned.
But the cowardly obit was already written:
Morning would know she was a common slut.

Russians who stood for tragedy
  Were sisters all around;
Dark conscience of the family, down she lay
To end the career of passion, brain a bruise;
And mother-wonder filled her like a tide,
Rabid and raging discipline to bear.

In came the monarchist, a nurse,
  And covered up her eyes;
Volkstaat of hate took over: suddenly
The Ego gagged, the Conscious overpowered,
The Memory beaten to a pulp, she fell.
It remained to hide the body, or make it laugh.

Yet not to sink her name in coin
  Like Caesar was her wish,
To come alive like Frick, conjecture maps,
Or speak with kings of low mentality,
But to be left alone, a law to scorn
Of all, and none more honored than the least.

This way she died, though premature
  Her clarity for others;
For it was taught that, listening, the soul
Lost track and merged with trespasses and spies
Whose black renown shook money like a rat
And showed up grass a mortmain property.

The Contraband

I dreamed I held a poem and knew
The capture of a living thing.
Boys in a Grecian circle sang
And women at their harvesting.

Slowly I tried to wake and draw
The vision after, word by word,
But sleep was covetous: the song
The singers and the singing blurred.

The paper flowers of everynight
All die. Day has no counterpart,
Where memory writes its boldface wish
And swiftly punishes the heart.

Construction

The confines of a city block
Cut to a monument, exact,
At all points rectilinear,
From air a perfect square intact,

As trim as Plato thought or Eu-
Clid drew with stick. What thinker put
This idea into cubes to sell
At fifty cents a cubic foot?

O neat, O dead, what feeling thing
Could buy so bare! O dead, O neat,
What beating heart could sink to buy
The copy of the die complete!

Blindmen

Consider them, my soul, the frightful blind!
Like mannikins, ridiculous, unbowed,
Singular, terrible, like somnambulists,
Darting their eyeballs overcast with cloud.

Their eyes from which the holy light has fled
As if far off they see, always look up;
Upon the stones of streets never look down
Inclining wearily their weighted heads. . . .

This way traverse the ever-enduring Dark,
Brother of Silence.—O Metropolis,
When all about you laugh and shout your song

With pleasure seized before this very wrong,
I cry, "I also drag myself behind!
What do they seek in Heaven, the truly blind?"

(Baudelaire translation)

Poet

Il arrive que l'esprit demande la poesie

Left leg flung out, head cocked to the right,
Tweed coat or army uniform, with book,
Beautiful eyes, who is this walking down?
Who, glancing at the pane of glass looks sharp
And thinks it is not he—as when a poet
Comes swiftly on some half-forgotten poem
And loosely holds the page, steady of mind,
   Thinking it is not his?

And when will *you* exist?—Oh, it is I,
Incredibly skinny, stooped, and neat as pie,
Ignorant as dirt, erotic as an ape,
Dreamy as puberty—with dirty hair!
Into the room like kangaroo he bounds,
Ears flopping like the most expensive hound's;
His chin receives all questions as he bows
   Mouthing a green bon-bon.

Has no more memory than rubber. Stands
Waist-deep in heavy mud of thought and broods
At his own wetness. When he would get out,
To his surprise he lifts in air a phrase
As whole and clean and silvery as a fish
Which jumps and dangles on his damned hooked grin,
But like a name-card on a man's lapel
   Calls him a conscious fool.

And child-like he remembers all his life
And cannily constructs it, fact by fact,
As boys paste postage stamps in careful books,
Denoting pence and legends and profiles,
Nothing more valuable.—And like a thief,
His eyes glassed over and congealed with guilt,
Fondles his secrets like a case of tools,
   And waits in empty doors.

By men despised for knowing what he is,
And by himself. But he exists for women.
As dolls to girls, as perfect wives to men,
So he to women. And to himself a thing,
All ages, epicene, without a trade.
To girls and wives always alive and fated;
To men and scholars always dead like Greek
        And always mistranslated.

Towards exile and towards shame he lures himself,
Tongue winding on his arm, and thinks like Eve
By biting apple will become most wise.
Sentio ergo sum: he feels his way
And words themselves stand up for him like Braille
And punch and perforate his parchment ear.
All language falls like Chinese on his soul,
        Image of song unsounded.

This is the coward's coward that in his dreams
Sees shapes of pain grow tall. Awake at night
He peers at sounds and stumbles at a breeze.
And none holds life less dear. For as a youth
Who by some accident observes his love
Naked and in some natural ugly act,
He turns with loathing and with flaming hands,
        Seared and betrayed by sight.

He is the business man, on beauty trades,
Dealer in arts and thoughts who, like the Jew,
Shall rise from slums and hated dialects
A tower of bitterness. Shall be always strange,
Hunted and then sought after. Shall be sat
Like an ambassador from another race
At tables rich with music. He shall eat flowers,
Chew honey and spit out gall. They shall all smile
        And love and pity him.

His death shall be by drowning. In that hour
When the last bubble of pure heaven's air
Hovers within his throat, safe on his bed,
A small eternal figurehead in terror,
He shall cry out and clutch his days of straw
Before the blackest wave. Lastly, his tomb
Shall list and founder in the troughs of grass
       And none shall speak his name.

Nostalgia

My soul stands at the window of my room,
    And I ten thousand miles away;
My days are filled with Ocean's sound of doom,
    Salt and cloud and the bitter spray.
Let the wind blow, for many a man shall die.

My selfish youth, my books with gilded edge,
    Knowledge and all gaze down the street;
The potted plants upon the window ledge
    Gaze down with selfish lives and sweet.
Let the wind blow, for many a man shall die.

My night is now her day, my day her night,
    So I lie down, and so I rise;
The sun burns close, the star is losing height,
    The clock is hunted down the skies.
Let the wind blow, for many a man shall die.

Truly a pin can make the memory bleed,
    A word explode the inward mind
And turn the skulls and flowers never freed
    Into the air, no longer blind.
Let the wind blow, for many a man shall die.

Laughter and grief join hands. Always the heart
    Clumps in the breast with heavy stride;
The face grows lined and wrinkled like a chart,
    The eyes bloodshot with tears and tide.
Let the wind blow, for many a man shall die.

from V-Letter and Other Poems

The Leg

Among the iodoform, in twilight-sleep,
What have I lost? he first inquires,
Peers in the middle distance where a pain,
Ghost of a nurse, hazily moves, and day,
Her blinding presence pressing in his eyes
And now his ears. They are handling him
With rubber hands. He wants to get up.

One day beside some flowers near his nose
He will be thinking, *When will I look at it?*
And pain, still in the middle distance, will reply,
At what? and he will know it's gone,
O where! and begin to tremble and cry.
He will begin to cry as a child cries
Whose puppy is mangled under a screaming wheel.

Later, as if deliberately, his fingers
Begin to explore the stump. He learns a shape
That is comfortable and tucked in like a sock.
This has a sense of humor, this can despise
The finest surgical limb, the dignity of limping,
The nonsense of wheel-chairs. Now he smiles to the wall:
The amputation becomes an acquisition.

For the leg is wondering where he is (all is not lost)
And surely he has a duty to the leg;
He is its injury, the leg is his orphan,
He must cultivate the mind of the leg,
Pray for the part that is missing, pray for peace
In the image of man, pray, pray for its safety,
And after a little it will die quietly.

The body, what is it, Father, but a sign
To love the force that grows us, to give back
What in Thy palm is senselessness and mud?
Knead, knead the substance of our understanding
Which must be beautiful in flesh to walk,
That if Thou take me angrily in hand
And hurl me to the shark, I shall not die!

The Interlude

I

Much of transfiguration that we hear,
The ballet of the atoms, the second law
Of thermo-dynamics, Isis, and the queer

Fertilization of fish, the Catholic's awe
For the life-cycle of the Nazarene,
His wife whom sleeping Milton thought he saw;

Much of the resurrection that we've seen
And taken part in, like the Passion Play,
All of autumnal red and April green,

To those who walk in work from day to day,
To economic and responsible man,
All, all is substance. Life that lets him stay

Uses his substance kindly while she can
But drops him lifeless after his one span.

II

What lives? the proper creatures in their homes?
A weed? the white and giddy butterfly?
Bacteria? necklaces of chromosomes?

What lives? the breathing bell of the clear sky?
The crazed bull of the sea? Andean crags?
Armies that plunge into themselves to die?

People? A sacred relic wrapped in rags,
The ham-bone of a saint, the winter rose,
Do these?—And is there not a hand that drags

The bottom of the universe for those
Who still perhaps are breathing? Listen well,
There lives a quiet like a cathedral close

At the soul's center where substance cannot dwell
And life flowers like music from a bell.

III

Writing, I crushed an insect with my nail
And thought nothing at all. A bit of wing
Caught my eye then, a gossamer so frail

And exquisite, I saw in it a thing
That scorned the grossness of the thing I wrote.
It hung upon my finger like a sting.

A leg I noticed next, fine as a mote,
"And on this frail eyelash he walked," I said,
"And climbed and walked like any mountain-goat."

And in this mood I sought the little head,
But it was lost; then in my heart a fear
Cried out, "A life—why beautiful, why dead!"

It was a mite that held itself most dear,
So small I could have drowned it with a tear.

The Synagogue

The synagogue dispirits the deep street,
Shadows the face of the pedestrian,
It is the adumbration of the Wall,
The stone survival that laments itself,
Our old entelechy of stubborn God,
Our calendar that marks a separate race.

The swift cathedral palpitates the blood,
The soul moves upward like a wing to meet
The pinnacles of saints. There flocks of thanks
In nooks of holy tracery arrive
And rested take their message in mid-air
Sphere after sphere into the papal heaven.

The altar of the Hebrews is a house,
No relic but a place, Sinai itself,
Not holy ground but factual holiness
Wherein the living god is resident.
Our scrolls are volumes of the thundered law
Sabbath by sabbath wound by hand to read.

He knows Al-Eloah to whom the Arab
Barefooted falls on sands, on table roofs,
In latticed alleys underneath the egg
On wide mosaics, when the crier shrills.
O profitable curse, most sacred rug,
Your book is blindness and your sword is rust.

And Judenhetze is the course of time;
We were rebellious, all but Abraham,
And skulked like Jonah, angry at the gourd.
Our days are captives in the minds of kings,
We stand in tens disjointed on the world
Grieving the ribbon of a coast we hated.

Some choose the ethics of belief beyond
Even particular election. Some
In bland memorial churches modify
The architecture of the state, and heaven
Disfranchised watches, caput mortuum,
The human substance eating, voting, smiling.

The Jew has no bedecked magnificat
But sits in stricken ashes after death,
Refusing grace; his grave is flowerless,
He gutters in the tallow of his name.
At Rome the multiplying tapers sing
Life endless in the history of art.

And Zion womanless refuses grace
To the first woman as to Magdalene,
But half-remembers Judith or Rahab,
The shrewd good heart of Esther honors still,
And weeps for almost sacred Ruth, but doubts
Either full harlotry or the faultless birth.

Our wine is wine, our bread is harvest bread
That feeds the body and is not the body.
Our blessing is to wine but not the blood
Nor to sangreal the sacred dish. We bless
The whiteness of the dish and bless the water
And are not anthropaphagous to him.

The immanent son then came as one of us
And stood against the ark. We have no prophets,
Our scholars are afraid. There have been friars,
Great healers, poets. The stars were terrible.
At the Sadducee court he touched our panic;
We were betrayed to sacrifice this man.

We live by virtue of philosophy,
Past love, and have our devious reward.
For faith he gave us land and took the land,
Thinking us exiles of all humankind.
Our name is yet the identity of God
That storms the falling altar of the world.

Shylock

Ho, no, no, no, no, my meaning in saying he is a good
man is to have you understand me, that he is sufficient.
                        —THE MERCHANT OF VENICE

Home from the court he locked the door and sat
In the evil darkness, suddenly composed.
The knife shone dimly on the table and his eyes
Like candles in an empty room
Shone hard at nothing. Yet he appeared to smile.

Then he took up his talith and his hat
And prayed mechanically and absently closed
His fingers on the knife. If he could realize
His actual defeat or personal doom
He must die or change or show that he was vile.

Nevertheless he would remain and live,
Submit to baptism, pay his fines,
Appear in the Rialto as early as tomorrow,
Not innocently but well aware
That his revenge is an accomplished fact.

And poverty itself would help to give
Humility to his old designs.
His fallen reputation would help borrow
A credit of new hate; for nothing will repair
This open breach of nature, cruel and wracked.

His daughter lies with swine, and the old rat
Tubal will be obsequious
To buy off his disgrace and bargain on his shame.
Despair can teach him nothing at all:
Gold he hates more than he hates Jesus' crown.

The logic of Balthasar will fall flat
On heaven's hearing. Incurious
As to the future, totally clear of blame,
He takes his ledgers out of the wall
And lights them with a taper and sits down.

Jew

The name is immortal but only the name, for the rest
Is a nose that can change in the weathers of time or persist
Or die out in confusion or model itself on the best.

But the name is a language itself that is whispered and hissed
Through the houses of ages, and ever a language the same,
And ever and ever a blow on our heart like a fist.

And this last of our dream in the desert, O curse of our name,
Is immortal as Abraham's voice in our fragment of prayer
Adonai, Adonai, for our bondage of murder and shame!

And the word for the murder of God will cry out on the air
Though the race is no more and the temples are closed of our will
And the peace is made fast on the earth and the earth is made fair;

Our name is impaled in the heart of the world on a hill
Where we suffer to die by the hands of ourselves, and to kill.

Nigger

And did ever a man go black with sun in a Belgian swamp,
On a feathery African plain where the sunburnt lioness lies,
And a cocoanut monkey grove where the cockatoos scratch
    the skies,
And the zebras striped with moonlight grasses gaze and stomp?

With a swatch of the baboon's crimson bottom cut for a lip,
And a brace of elephant ivories hung for a tusky smile,
With the muscles as level and lazy and long as the lifting Nile,
And a penis as loaded and supple and limp as the slaver's whip?

Are you beautiful still when you walk downtown in a knife-
    cut coat
And your yellow shoes dance at the corner curb like a brand-
    new car,
And the buck with the arching pick looks over the new-laid tar
As you cock your eye like a cuckoo bird on a two-o'clock note?

When you got so little in steel-rim specs, when you taught
    that French,
When you wrote that book and you made that speech in the
    bottom south,
When you beat that fiddle and sang that role for Othello's
    mouth,
When you blew that horn for the shirt-sleeve mob and the
    snaky wench?

When you boxed that hun, when you raped that trash that
    you didn't rape,
When you caught that slug with a belly of fire and a face of
    gray,
When you felt that loop and you took that boot from a KKK,
And your hands hung down and your face went out in a
    blast of grape?

Did the Lord say yes, did the Lord say no, did you ask the Lord
When the jaw came down, when the cotton blossomed out of
    your bones?
Are you coming to peace, O Booker T. Lincoln Roosevelt Jones,
And is Jesus riding to raise your wage and to cut that cord?

Troop Train

It stops the town we come through. Workers raise
Their oily arms in good salute and grin.
Kids scream as at a circus. Business men
Glance hopefully and go their measured way.
And women standing at their dumbstruck door
More slowly wave and seem to warn us back,
As if a tear blinding the course of war
Might once dissolve our iron in their sweet wish.

Fruit of the world, O clustered on ourselves
We hang as from a cornucopia
In total friendliness, with faces bunched
To spray the streets with catcalls and with leers.
A bottle smashes on the moving ties
And eyes fixed on a lady smiling pink
Stretch like a rubber-band and snap and sting
The mouth that wants the drink-of-water kiss.

And on through crummy continents and days,
Deliberate, grimy, slightly drunk we crawl,
The good-bad boys of circumstance and chance,
Whose bucket-helmets bang the empty wall
Where twist the murdered bodies of our packs
Next to the guns that only seem themselves.
And distance like a strap adjusted shrinks,
Tighten across the shoulder and holds firm.

Here is a deck of cards; out of this hand
Dealer, deal me my luck, a pair of bulls,
The right draw to a flush, the one-eyed jack.
Diamonds and hearts are red but spades are black,
And spades are spades and clubs are clovers—black.
But deal me winners, souvenirs of peace.
This stands to reason and arithmetic,
Luck also travels and not all come back.

Trains lead to ships and ships to death or trains,
And trains to death or trucks, and trucks to death,
Or trucks lead to the march, the march to death,
Or that survival which is all our hope;
And death leads back to trucks and trains and ships,
But life leads to the march, O flag! at last
The place of life found after trains and death—
Nightfall of nations brilliant after war.

Full Moon: New Guinea

These nights we fear the aspects of the moon,
Sleep lightly in the radiance falling clear
On palms and ferns and hills and us; for soon
The small burr of the bombers in our ear
Tickles our rest; we rise as from a nap
And take our helmets absently and meet,
Prepared for any spectacle or mishap,
At trenches fresh and narrow at our feet.

Look up, look up, and wait and breathe. These nights
We fear Orion and the Cross. The crowd
Of deadly insects caught in our long lights
Glitter and seek to burrow in a cloud
Soft-minded with high explosive. Breathe and wait,
The bombs are falling darkly for our fate.

The Gun

You were angry and manly to shatter the sleep of your throat;
The kiss of your blast is upon me, O friend of my fear,
And I savour your breath like a perfume as salt and austere
As the scent of the thunder of heaven that brims in the moat!

I grip you. We lie on the ground in the thongs of our clasp
And we stare like the hunter who starts at a tenuous cry;
We have wounded the wind with a wire and stung in the sky
A white hole that is small and unseen as the bite of the asp.

The smooth of your cheek—Do you sight from the depth of
    your eye
More faultless than vision, more true than the aiming of stars?
Is the heart of your hatred the target of redness of Mars
Or the roundness of heart of the one who must stumble and die?

O the valley is silent and shocked. I absolve from your name
The exaction of murder, my gun. It is I who have killed.
It is I whose enjoyment of horror is fine and fulfilled.
You are only the toy of my terror, my emblem of blame.

Come with me. We shall creep for his eyes like the sweat of
    my skin,
For the wind is repaired and the fallen is calling for breath.
You are only the means of the practical humor of death
Which is savage to punish the dead for the sake of my sin!

Sunday: New Guinea

The bugle sounds the measured call to prayers,
The band starts bravely with a clarion hymn,
From every side, singly, in groups, in pairs,
Each to his kind of service comes to worship Him.

Our faces washed, our hearts in the right place,
We kneel or stand or listen from our tents;
Half-naked natives with their kind of grace
Move down the road with balanced staffs like mendicants.

And over the hill the guns bang like a door
And planes repeat their mission in the heights.
The jungle outmaneuvers creeping war
And crawls within the circle of our sacred rites.

I long for our disheveled Sundays home,
Breakfast, the comics, news of latest crimes,
Talk without reference, and palindromes,
Sleep and the Philharmonic and the ponderous *Times*.

I long for lounging in the afternoons
Of clean intelligent warmth, my brother's mind,
Books and thin plates and flowers and shining spoons,
And your love's presence, snowy, beautiful, and kind.

Fireworks

In midsummer darkness when primeval silences close
On the women in linen and children and husbands in blouses
We gather in laughter and move with a current that flows
Through the intimate suburbs of ice-cream and talkative houses

To a fabulous field of the night of the rainbows of ages
Where blindness is dyed with the blooms and the tints of desire,
And the wars of our boyhood rise up from the oldest of pages
With heroes erected on billboards of fuses and wire.

In the garden of pleistocene flowers we wander like Alice
Where seed sends a stalk in the heavens and pops from a pod
A blue blossom that hangs on the distance and opens its chalice
And falls in the dust of itself and goes out with a nod.

How the hairy tarantulas crawl in the soft of the ether
Where showers of lilies explode in the jungle of creepers;
How the rockets of sperm hurtle up to the moon and beneath her
Deploy for the eggs of the astral and sorrowful sleepers!

And the noble bombardment that bursts in the depth of our ears
Lifts the hair of our heads and interprets in absolute noises
The brimstone of total destruction, the doom of our years.
O the Judgment that shatters the rose of our secrets and poises!

In Niagaras of fire we leak in the luminous aura
And gasp at the portrait of Lincoln alive on the lattice.
Our history hisses and spits in the burning Gomorrah,
The volcanoes subside; we are given our liberty gratis.

Satire: Anxiety

Alas, I would be overloved,
A sign, a Wonder unreproved,
A bronze colossus standing high
As Rhodes or famous Liberty,
Bridging with my almighty thighs
A stainless-steel metropolis
Where pigmy men in clothing creep
To Lilliputian work and sleep,
And Love with microscopic tears
Whispers to wee and perfect ears.
I would obscure the sun and throw
A shadow with my smallest toe
That down their teeming canyon files
Time could be told a hundred miles;
Lightning would flash within my hand,
An airman's beacon and sign of land,
My eyes eclipse the polar star,
Aldebaran and the flare of war;
Golden my head and cleanly hewn
Would sail above the lesser moon
And dart above the Pleiades
To peer at new astronomies
From where the earth, a bluish clod,
Seems smallest in the eye of God.

But when in lucid morning I
Survey my bulk and history,
Composite fool alive in air
With caecum and vestigial hair,
A thing of not-too-godly form
Conversant with the waiting worm,
Fixed in a span between two shades
For four or five or six decades,
Then all my pride and all my hope

As backward through a telescope
Diminish: I walk an endless street
Where topless towers for height compete,
And men of wiser blood and bone
Destroy me for the things they own—
Their taxes, vital tubes, and sons
Submissive in a world of guns.
I see my hands grow small and clear
Until they wink and disappear.

The Bed

Your clothes of snow and satin and pure blood
Are surplices of many sacraments
Full of the woven musk of birth and death,
Full of the wet wild-flower breath of marriages,
The sweat, the slow mandragora of lust.

Meadow of sleep, table of sour sickness,
Infinite road to travel, first of graves,
Your square and subtle presence rules the house,
And little wincing hurts of everyday
Clutch at your white skirt and are comforted.

What matter if you are wise or if you know?
A third of life is yours, all that we learn
We tell you, and you dream us night by night.
We take your advice, confess in sharp detail,
Add to your knowledge, yet can teach you nothing.
"Lie here," you say, and whoever we bring you, sad,
Ashamed or delighted, you take in the spirit we give.

Let me not know too much, and let your soul
Not lead me farther on than sleep and love,
For her I marry is more white than you.
Some day, as if with ancient torches stand
And fill the walls with fires around her head,
And let your gown be fresh as April grass,
And let your prothalamium be sweet.

The Second-Best Bed

In the name of the almighty God, amen,
  I, William Shakespeare, take my pen
  And do bequeath in perfect health
To Christ my soul and to my kin my wealth
      When I am dead.
      And to Anne, good dame,
      I bequeath my name,
A table, a chair, and the second-best bed.

To Judith a hundred fifty pounds I give,
  The same if three more years she live,
  And the broad-edge silver bowl. To Joan
My hose and clothes and all the suits I own
      Both blue and red.
      And to Anne, good dame,
      I bequeath my name,
A table, a chair, and the second-best bed.

Ten pounds to beggars for their drink and board,
  To Mr. Thomas Cole my sword,
  To Richard Burbage, Cundell, Nash,
Heminge and Hamlet one pound six in cash,
      And to her I wed
      Who is Anne, good dame,
      I bequeath my name,
A table, a chair, and the second-best bed.

To Joan also my Stratford house I will,
  For sisters shall not go with nil,
  And to her sons five pounds apiece
To be paid within a year of my decease.
      And as I have said
      To Anne, good dame,
      I bequeath my name,
A table, a chair, and the second-best bed.

Last, to my daughter, born Susanna Hall,
    My barns and stables, lands and all,
    Tenements, orchards, jewels, and wares,
All these forever for herself and heirs,
        Till all are dead;
        But to Anne, good dame,
        I bequeath my name,
A table, a chair, and the second-best bed.

Good wife, bad fortune is to blame
That I bequeath, when I am dead,
To you my honor and my name,
A table, a chair, and the second-best bed.

Magician

Tall in his top hat, tall and alone in the room
Of aerial music, electric light
And the click of tables, the mephistophelian man
Toys with a wand and the wonders happen—for whom
And to what end the gleam of the shellacked
Trick within trick, as plain as black and white,
And all too clever, all too matter-of-fact
Like the sudden neatness of a shutting fan?

And somewhat sinister, like a millionaire
Or a poet or a street-corner quack
With a dollar bottle of cure . . . We are drawn to his eye
Only to stop at the eye we dare not dare;
We suspect and believe; *he* looks us out of face
And seems to say that magic is the knack
Of showing the result without a trace
Of the cause, end without means, what without why.

If now the amusing audience could see
His mangey unicorn that crops
The shabby velvet of his weariness,
An inch from the abyss of villainy,
The applause would freeze, the dust settle like snow,
And long before the asbestos curtain drops
Even the children would get up to go,
Be sick in the lobby, sob with young distress;

But fortunately they cannot. We proceed
Beyond the fire-eating, doves,
Padlocks, confetti, disappearing ropes,
To personal murder, the necessary deed
Of sawing a woman in half. We want her heart.
The sable executioner in gloves
Labors, but hoc est corpus! quite apart
She stands; we applaud our disappointed hopes.

And backstage somewhere, peeling his moustache,
He muses that he is an honest man
And wonders dramatically why. Deep in his ear
At times there sounds the subterranean plash
Of Alf and Phlegeton where tides revolve
With eyes of evil. There he first began;
There is the task he can no longer solve
But only wait for till his dying year.

Red Indian

To Jim Powell

Purest of breed of all the tribes
That trekked from time and took the Trail of Tears
There to the plain beyond the bribes
Of best advantage, past the rifle's reach,
Where instinct rests and action disappears
And the skulls of cattle bleach.

High in the plateaus of their soul
The silence is reshaped like rocks by wind,
Their eyes are beads that pay their toll,
Record the race-long heritage of grief,
At altitudes where memory is thinned,
Frown like a wrinkled chief.

The painted feather still upright
They walk in concrete Tulsa dark and mute,
Their bravest blankets slashing bright
The afternoon of progress and of wives;
Their children glow like some primordial fruit
Cut from the branch by knives.

Bark-smooth as spears and arrow-straight
They watch the world like winter trees and grow;
Forests of them revive and wait,
In timeless hibernation dream and stir.
These are the lives that love the soundless snow
And wear the wind like fur.

Because their pride of nation leaps,
The august rivers where they yelled and died
Move with a blood that never sleeps.
Because their nature suffers the arrest
Of seed, their silence crowds us like a tide
And moves their mournful quest.

Sydney Bridge

Though I see you, O rainbow of iron and rivetted lace
As a dancer who leaps to the music of music and light,
And poised on the pin of the moment of marvelous grace
Holds her breath in the downfall and curve of her motionless
     flight;

Though you walk like a queen with the stays of your womanly
     steel
And the pearls of your bodice are heavy with sensual pride,
And the million come under your notice and graciously kneel,
As the navies of nations come slowly to moor at your side;

Yet your pace is the pace of a man's, and your arms are out-
     spread
In a trick of endurance to charm the demand of the bays,
And your tendons are common—the cables are coarse on your
     head,

You are marxist and sweaty! You grind for the labor of days;
And O sphinx of our harbor of beauty, your banner is red
And outflung at the end of the world like a silvery phrase!

Piano

The perfect ice of the thin keys must break
And fingers crash through stillness into sound,
And through the mahogany darkness of the lake
Splinter the muteness where all notes are found.
O white face floating upwards amidst hair!
Sweet hands entangled in the golden snare,
       Escape, escape, escape,
    Or in the coils of joy be drowned.

What is the cabinet that holds such speech
And is obedient to caresses strange
As tides that stroke the long-deserted beach,
And gales that scourge the Peruvian mountain range?
O flesh of wood with flanks aglow with suns,
O quivering as at the burst of monstrous guns,
       Subside, subside, subside,
    Or into dust and atoms change.

Nor can the note-shaped heart, nor can the ear
Withstand your praise, O numbers more appalling
Than ringed and voyaging on the atmosphere
Those heavy flocks of fallen angels falling;
You strike with fists of heaven against the void
Where all but choiring music is destroyed,
       And light, and light, and light,
    Bursts into voice forever calling.

Christmas Eve: Australia

The wind blows hot. English and foreign birds
And insects different as their fish excite
The would-be calm. The usual flocks and herds
Parade in permanent quiet out of sight,
And there one crystal like a grain of light
Sticks in the crucible of day and cools.
A cloud burnt to a crisp at some great height
Sips at the dark condensing in deep pools.

I smoke and read my Bible and chew gum,
Thinking of Christ and Christmas of last year,
And what those quizzical soldiers standing near
Ask of the war and Christmases to come,
And sick of causes and the tremendous blame
Curse lightly and pronounce your serious name.

Hill at Parramatta

Just like a wave, the long green hill of my desire
Rides to the shore-like level here to engulf us all
Who work and joke in the hollow grave and the shallow mire
Where we must dig or else the earth will truly fall.

Long as a comber, green as grass, taut as a tent,
And there far out like specks the browsing cattle drift,
And sweet sweet with the green of life and the downhill scent,
O sweet at the heart such heavy loveliness to lift!

And you know best the void of the world, the blue and green,
And the races departing single file to the west to die—
But all your memory shines on the tiny deaths you have seen
No more nor less than the point of light in the tear of my eye:

So proud of the wave, my womanly hill, to lean on the shore
And tumble the sands and flatness of death with your silent roar.

Melbourne

The planted palms will keep the city warm
In any winter, and the toy Yarra flow
With boats and lovers down the grass. From walls
The flowers spring to sack the very streets
And wrought-iron tendrils curl upon the air.
The family's sex is English, and all their pain
More moderate than a long-expected death.

Yet the lipstick is poor, the girls consent
To lose their teeth and hips, and language whines
Raising the pitch to shrill humility.
At five o'clock the pubs roar on the world
And milk bars trickle pardon, as the mobs
Lunge, worse than Chicago, for the trains
Dispersing life to gardens and to tea.

Also in suburbs there is want of vice,
And even the dogs are well-behaved and nice.
Who has extracted violence like the fang,
Leaving in early minds the simile
Castration? Who watching at night the film
Suffers the technicolor King to spread
Exalted, motionless, into their dream?

For blue and diluted is this nation's eye,
Wind-worn with herding and great distances
That were not made for cities. This was a land
Laid for the park of loneliness of Earth,
And giant imagination and despair.
Who reared this sweet metropolis abides
By his own error, more profound than war.

Only my love can spare the wasted race
That worships sullenly the sordid sheep.
She shall be governor with her golden hair!
And teach the landscape laughter and destroy
With her free naked foot the matchwood quay:
Buildings themselves shall topple where she dances
And leap like frogs into the uproarious sea!

V-Letter

I love you first because your face is fair,
>   Because your eyes Jewish and blue,
Set sweetly with the touch of foreignness
Above the cheekbones, stare rather than dream.
Often your countenance recalls a boy
>   Blue-eyed and small, whose silent mischief
Tortured his parents and compelled my hate
>   To wish his ugly death.
Because of this reminder, my soul's trouble,
And for your face, so often beautiful,
>   I love you, wish you life.

I love you first because you wait, because
>   For your own sake, I cannot write
Beyond these words. I love you for these words
That sting and creep like insects and leave filth.
I love you for the poverty you cry
>   And I bend down with tears of steel
That melt your hand like wax, not for this war
>   The droplets shattering
Those candle-glowing fingers of my joy,
But for your name of agony, my love,
>   That cakes my mouth with salt.

And all your imperfections and perfections
>   And all your magnitude of grace
And all this love explained and unexplained
Is just a breath. I see you woman-size
And this looms larger and more goddess-like
>   Than silver goddesses on screens.
I see you in the ugliness of light,
>   Yet you are beautiful,
And in the dark of absence your full length
Is such as meets my body to the full
>   Though I am starved and huge.

You turn me from these days as from a scene
      Out of an open window far
Where lies the foreign city and the war.
You are my home and in your spacious love
I dream to march as under flaring flags
      Until the door is gently shut.
Give me the tearless lesson of your pride,
        Teach me to live and die
As one deserving anonymity,
The mere devotion of a house to keep
      A woman and a man.

Give me the free and poor inheritance
      Of our own kind, not furniture
Of education, nor the prophet's pose,
The general cause of words, the hero's stance,
The ambitions incommensurable with flesh,
      But the drab makings of a room
Where sometimes in the afternoon of thought
        The brief and blinding flash
May light the enormous chambers of your will
And show the gracious Parthenon that time
      Is ever measured by.

As groceries in a pantry gleam and smile
      Because they are important weights
Bought with the metal minutes of your pay,
So do these hours stand in solid rows,
The dowry for a use in common life.
      I love you first because your years
Lead to my matter-of-fact and simple death
        Or to our open marriage,
And I pray nothing for my safety back,
Not even luck, because our love is whole
      Whether I live or fail.

Lord, I Have Seen Too Much

Lord, I have seen too much for one who sat
In quiet at his window's luminous eye
And puzzled over house and street and sky,
Safe only in the narrowest habitat;
Who studied peace as if the world were flat,
The edge of nature linear and dry,
But faltered at each brilliant entity
Drawn like a prize from some magician's hat.

Too suddenly this lightning is disclosed:
Lord, in a day the vacuum of Hell,
The mouth of blood, the ocean's ragged jaw,
More than embittered Adam ever saw
When driven from Eden to the East to dwell,
The lust of godhead hideously exposed!

Franklin

The star of Reason, Ben, reposed in you
Octagon spectacles, a sparking kite,
Triggers and jiggers, bobbins, reels and screws,
And aphorisms spelled in black and white.

Wiseacre, editor, and diplomat,
First of the salesmen, hero of the clerk,
The logic of invention led to bells
Joyous for George and terrible for Burke.

Poor Richard prospers and the grocery man
Has your disarming prose and pays his tax.
Sir, what is the reason for this bird
That sings and screams and coos and crows and quacks?

Two-penny buns, a whistle for the boy,
Rare Ben, the printer's devil used you well.
Lenin and Freud embroider left and right
And Curtis beats The Independence Bell.

Jefferson

If vision can dilate, my noble lord,
Farther than porticos, Italian cells,
Newtonian gardens, Haydn, and cuisine,
Tell us, most serious of all our poets,
Why is the clock so low?

I see the tender gradient of your will;
Virginia is the Florence of your soul,
Yes, ours. The architecture of your hands
Quiets ambition and revives our skill
And buys our faithlessness.

So temperate, so remote, so sure of phrase,
Your music sweeps a continent, a sphere,
Fashions a modern language for a war
And by its cadence makes responsible
Our million names to you.

When you were old the god of government
Seemed to recede a pace, and you were glad.
You watched the masons through your telescope
Finish your school of freedom. Death itself
Stood thoughtful at your bed.

And now the surfaces of mind are rubbed
Our essence starts like serum from our eyes.
How can you not assume the deities
That move behind the bloodshot look and lean
Like saints and Salem devils?

Ballet Mécanique

The hand involves the wheel that weaves the hand
Without the kiss of kind; the digits flick,
The cranks obedient to no command
Raise on their iron shoulders the dead weight
For which no forges cheer. Nothing is late,
Nothing behind, excited, or too quick.
The arm involves the treadle and the wheel
Winds wakeless motion on a tireless reel.

The kiss of kind remembers wood and wool
To no cold purpose, anciently, afar:
The wheel forgets the hand that palpitates
The danceless power, and the power waits
Coiled in the tension tower for the pull
That freezes the burnt hand upon the bar.

The Intellectual

What should the wars do with these jigging fools?

The man behind the book may not be man,
His own man or the book's or yet the time's,
But still be whole, deciding what he can
In praise of politics or German rimes;

But the intellectual lights a cigarette
And offers it lit to the lady, whose odd smile
Is the merest hyphen—lest he should forget
What he has been resuming all the while.

He talks to overhear, she to withdraw
To some interior feminine fireside
Where the back arches, beauty puts forth a paw
Like a black puma stretching in velvet pride,

Making him think of cats, a stray of which
Some days sets up a howling in his brain,
Pure interference such as this neat bitch
Seems to create from listening disdain.

But talk is all the value, the release,
Talk is the very fillip of an act,
The frame and subject of the masterpiece
Under whose film of age the face is cracked.

His own forehead glows like expensive wood,
But back of it the mind is disengaged,
Self-sealing clock recording bad and good
At constant temperature, intact, unaged.

But strange, his body is an open house
Inviting every passerby to stay;
The city to and fro beneath his brows
Wanders and drinks and chats from night to day.

Think of a private thought, indecent room
Where one might kiss his daughter before bed!
Life is embarrassed; shut the family tomb,
Console your neighbor for his recent dead;

Do something! die in Spain or paint a green
Gouache, go into business (Rimbaud did),
Or start another Little Magazine,
Or move in with a woman, have a kid.

Invulnerable, impossible, immune,
Do what you will, your will will not be done
But dissipate the light of afternoon
Till evening flickers like the midnight sun,

And midnight shouts and dies: I'd rather be
A milkman walking in his sleep at dawn
Bearing fat quarts of cream, and so be free,
Crossing alone and cold from lawn to lawn.

I'd rather be a barber and cut hair
Than walk with you in gilt museum halls,
You and the puma-lady, she so rare
Exhaling her silk soul upon the walls.

Go take yourselves apart, but let me be
The fault you find with everyman. I spit,
I laugh, I fight; and you, *l'homme qui rît*,
Swallow your stale saliva, and still sit.

Elegy for a Dead Soldier

I

A white sheet on the tail-gate of a truck
Becomes an altar; two small candlesticks
Sputter at each side of the crucifix
Laid round with flowers brighter than the blood,
Red as the red of our apocalypse,
Hibiscus that a marching man will pluck
To stick into his rifle or his hat,
And great blue morning-glories pale as lips
That shall no longer taste or kiss or swear.
The wind begins a low magnificat,
The chaplain chats, the palmtrees swirl their hair,
The columns come together through the mud.

II

We too are ashes as we watch and hear
The psalm, the sorrow, and the simple praise
Of one whose promised thoughts of other days
Were such as ours, but now wholly destroyed,
The service record of his youth wiped out,
His dream dispersed by shot, must disappear.
What can we feel but wonder at a loss
That seems to point at nothing but the doubt
Which flirts our sense of luck into the ditch?
Reader of Paul who prays beside this fosse,
Shall we believe our eyes or legends rich
With glory and rebirth beyond the void?

III

For this comrade is dead, dead in the war,
A young man out of millions yet to live,
One cut away from all that war can give,
Freedom of self and peace to wander free.
Who mourns in all this sober multitude

Who did not feel the bite of it before
The bullet found its aim? This worthy flesh,
This boy laid in a coffin and reviewed—
Who has not wrapped himself in this same flag,
Heard the light fall of dirt, his wound still fresh,
Felt his eyes closed, and heard the distant brag
Of the last volley of humanity?

IV

By chance I saw him die, stretched on the ground,
A tattooed arm lifted to take the blood
Of someone else sealed in a tin. I stood
During the last delirium that stays
The intelligence a tiny moment more,
And then the strangulation, the last sound.
The end was sudden, like a foolish play,
A stupid fool slamming a foolish door,
The absurd catastrophe, half-prearranged,
And all the decisive things still left to say.
So we disbanded, angrier and unchanged,
Sick with the utter silence of dispraise.

V

We ask for no statistics of the killed,
For nothing political impinges on
This single casualty, or all those gone,
Missing or healing, sinking or dispersed,
Hundreds of thousands counted, millions lost.
More than an accident and less than willed
Is every fall, and this one like the rest.
However others calculate the cost,
To us the final aggregate is *one*,
One with a name, one transferred to the blest;
And though another stoops and takes the gun,
We cannot add the second to the first.

VI

I would not speak for him who could not speak
Unless my fear were true: he was not wronged,

He knew to which decision he belonged
But let it choose itself. Ripe in instinct,
Neither the victim nor the volunteer,
He followed, and the leaders could not seek
Beyond the followers. Much of this he knew;
The journey was a detour that would steer
Into the Lincoln Highway of a land
Remorselessly improved, excited, new,
And that was what he wanted. He had planned
To earn and drive. He and the world had winked.

VII

No history deceived him, for he knew
Little of times and armies not his own;
He never felt that peace was but a loan,
Had never questioned the idea of gain.
Beyond the headlines once or twice he saw
The gathering of a power by the few
But could not tell their names; he cast his vote,
Distrusting all the elected but not law.
He laughed at socialism; *on mourrait*
Pour les industriels? He shed his coat
And not for brotherhood, but for his pay.
To him the red flag marked the sewer main.

VIII

Above all else he loathed the homily,
The slogan and the ad. He paid his bill,
But not for Congressmen at Bunker Hill.
Ideals were few and those there were not made
For conversation. He belonged to church
But never spoke of God. The Christmas tree,
The Easter egg, baptism, he observed,
Never denied the preacher on his perch,
And would not sign Resolved That or Whereas.
Softness he had and hours and nights reserved
For thinking, dressing, dancing to the jazz.
His laugh was real, his manners were homemade.

IX

Of all men poverty pursued him least;
He was ashamed of all the down and out,
Spurned the panhandler like an uneasy doubt,
And saw the unemployed as a vague mass
Incapable of hunger or revolt.
He hated other races, south or east,
And shoved them to the margin of his mind.
He could recall the justice of the Colt,
Take interest in a gang-war like a game.
His ancestry was somewhere far behind
And left him only his peculiar name.
Doors opened, and he recognized no class.

X

His children would have known a heritage,
Just or unjust, the richest in the world,
The quantum of all art and science curled
In the horn of plenty, bursting from the horn,
A people bathed in honey, Paris come,
Vienna transferred with the highest wage,
A World's Fair spread to Phoenix, Jacksonville,
Earth's capital, the new Byzantium,
Kingdom of man—who knows? Hollow or firm,
No man can ever prophesy until
Out of our death some undiscovered germ,
Whole toleration or pure peace is born.

XI

The time to mourn is short that best becomes
The military dead. We lift and fold the flag,
Lay bare the coffin with its written tag,
And march away. Behind, four others wait
To lift the box, the heaviest of loads.
The anesthetic afternoon benumbs,
Sickens our senses, forces back our talk.
We know that others on tomorrow's roads
Will fall, ourselves perhaps, the man beside,

Over the world the threatened, all who walk:
And could we mark the grave of him who died
We would write this beneath his name and date:

EPITAPH

Underneath this wooden cross there lies
A Christian killed in battle. You who read,
Remember that this stranger died in pain;
And passing here, if you can lift your eyes
Upon a peace kept by a human creed,
Know that one soldier has not died in vain.

from Essay on Rime

The Dead Hand and Exhaustion of Our Rime

With the instinctive vigilance of the great
Explorer, Freud in a final summary
Of psychoanalysis as a key to life
Denies its value as a Weltanschauung.
The founder of depth psychology disavowing
Philosophy and religion as the mummery
Of wishfulness and illusion turns at last
To total science as the remaining basis
For whole belief; nor does he minimize
The force and the persistence of past faiths
And present in the psychic scheme of things.
But of the arts—and here we end our tract
On rime—he briefly says that in the main
They are beneficent and harmless forms.
This is the sane perspective, one that brings
The beloved creative function back to scale.
We cannot end like Dante on the stars
Until we view them with the saintly gaze
Of humble men acknowledging our knowledge
Of nothing. Though we pretend to walk on Mars
With its proposed canals, Platonic cities
And supermen, while in the grip of art
As Weltanschauung, we show that we have failed
To cross the neutral void. Secure on earth,
The rime of pure belief, its spirit spent,
Tired, hysterical, diffuse and vain,
Beseeches such as Freud for sympathy
And is rejected. Ultimately, on pain
Of violent separation from the states
Of being, art in its disembodied forms
Wanders through life as through a mardigras
And maunders back upon the stroke of twelve
To black oblivion. Reconstructing night,
The poet with painted and lack-lustre eye

Stares in the glass at pallid dawn and sees
The image of his sufficiency, a face
Wretched in weakness and a vibrant claw
Trailing a pen. From such ennui the poem
Takes its first line, digresses for a space,
Slips sidewise on a metaphor, proceeds
In doubt of its intention toward a pitch
Of mild mental excitement, strings its beads
Of meaning on the mended thread of rhythm,
Comments its way to a conclusion which
Is nothing but the vestigial proof of nothing;
Or else in senseless violence on itself
Ends in a brawl of vocatives and a roar
Of "ancestral voices prophesying war."
This is the norm and type of modern rime
In the mid-century of our art; deny
The evidence if you will, but there are tiers
Of volumes marked and catalogued and sealed
At library temperature, and enough to lay
A crowd of us forever in Potter's Field.
I do not mean to fix an epitaph
To this essay, or end on the dead note
Of disillusion. Lucky for all concerned
No man can kill the destined poem or breathe
A breath into the natural corpse of one.
To feel the stir of life, impounded sun
In rime is finally the pragmatic test;
Nor can we take the measure of the best
Except for our own time. In the long run
The crimes and fallacies of an age of art
Are set beside its high deeds and its truths
In reasonable perspective. Not to stand pat
On this truism, however, or break the back
Of my own cause, I here should underline
The three confusions I have spoken of,
In Prosody, in Language, and in Belief.
That these aspects should terminate in grief
To art is our misfortune. In the above

I have tried to indicate no more than that
The aftermath of poetry should be love.

from Trial of a Poet

The Dirty Word

The dirty word hops in the cage of the mind like the Pondi-cherry vulture, stomping with its heavy left claw on the sweet meat of the brain and tearing it with its vicious beak, ripping and chopping the flesh. Terrified, the small boy bears the big bird of the dirty word into the house, and grunting, puffing, carries it up the stairs to his own room in the skull. Bits of black feather cling to his clothes and his hair as he locks the staring creature in the dark closet.

All day the small boy returns to the closet to examine and feed the bird, to caress and kick the bird, that now snaps and flaps its wings savagely whenever the door is opened. How the boy trembles and delights at the sight of the white excre-ment of the bird! How the bird leaps and rushes against the walls of the skull, trying to escape from the zoo of the vocab-ulary! How wildly snaps the sweet meat of the brain in its rage.

And the bird outlives the man, being freed at the man's death-funeral by a word from the rabbi.

But I one morning went upstairs and opened the door and entered the closet and found in the cage of my mind the great bird dead. Softly I wept it and softly removed it and softly buried the body of the bird in the hollyhock garden of the house I lived in twenty years before. And out of the worn black feathers of the wing have I made pens to write these elegies, for I have outlived the bird, and I have murdered it in my early manhood.

Homecoming

Lost in the vastness of the void Pacific
My thousand days of exile, pain,
Bid me farewell. Gone is the Southern Cross
To her own sky, fallen a continent
Under the wave, dissolved the bitterest isles
In their salt element,
And here upon the deck the mist encloses
My smile that would light up all darkness
And ask forgiveness of the things that thrust
Shame and all death on millions and on me.

We bring no raw materials from the East
But green-skinned men in blue-lit holds
And lunatics impounded between-decks;
The mighty ghoul-ship that we ride exhales
The sickly-sweet stench of humiliation,
And even the majority, untouched by steel
Or psychoneurosis, stare with eyes in rut,
Their hands a rabble to snatch the riches
Of glittering shops and girls.

Because I am angry at this kindness which
Is both habitual and contradictory
To the life of armies, now I stand alone
And hate the swarms of khaki men that crawl
Like lice upon the wrinkled hide of earth,
Infesting ships as well. Not otherwise
Could I lean outward piercing fog to find
Our sacred bridge of exile and return.
My tears are psychological, not poems
To the United States; my smile is prayer.

Gnawing the thin slops of anxiety,
Escorted by the ground swell and by gulls,
In silence and with mystery we enter
The territorial waters. Not till then
Does that convulsive terrible joy, more sudden
And brilliant than the explosion of a ship,
Shatter the tensions of the heaven and sea
To crush a hundred thousand skulls
And liberate in that high burst of love
The imprisoned souls of soldiers and of me.

The Conscientious Objector

The gates clanged and they walked you into jail
More tense than felons but relieved to find
The hostile world shut out, the flags that dripped
From every mother's windowpane, obscene
The bloodlust sweating from the public heart,
The dog authority slavering at your throat.
A sense of quiet, of pulling down the blind
Possessed you. Punishment you felt was clean.

The decks, the catwalks, and the narrow light
Composed a ship. This was a mutinous crew
Troubling the captains for plain decencies,
A Mayflower brim with pilgrims headed out
To establish new theocracies to west,
A Noah's ark coasting the topmost seas
Ten miles above the sodomites and fish.
These inmates loved the only living doves.

Like all men hunted from the world you made
A good community, voyaging the storm
To no safe Plymouth or green Ararat;
Trouble or calm, the men with Bibles prayed,
The gaunt politicals construed our hate.
The opposite of all armies, you were best
Opposing uniformity and yourselves;
Prison and personality were your fate.

You suffered not so physically but knew
Maltreatment, hunger, ennui of the mind.
Well might the soldier kissing the hot beach
Erupting in his face damn all your kind.
Yet you who saved neither yourselves nor us
Are equally with those who shed the blood
The heroes of our cause. Your conscience is
What we come back to in the armistice.

The Progress of Faust

He was born in Deutschland, as you would suspect,
And graduated in magic from Cracow
In Fifteen Five. His portraits show a brow
Heightened by science. The eye is indirect,
As of bent light upon a crooked soul,
And that he bargained with the Prince of Shame
For pleasures intellectually foul
Is known by every court that lists his name.

His frequent disappearances are put down
To visits in the regions of the damned
And to the periodic deaths he shammed,
But, unregenerate and in Doctor's gown,
He would turn up to lecture at the fair
And do a minor miracle for a fee.
Many a life he whispered up the stair
To teach the black art of anatomy.

He was as deaf to angels as an oak
When, in the fall of Fifteen Ninety-four,
He went to London and crashed through the floor
In mock damnation of the playgoing folk.
Weekending with the scientific crowd,
He met Sir Francis Bacon and helped draft
"Colours of Good and Evil" and read aloud
An obscene sermon at which no one laughed.

He toured the Continent for a hundred years
And subsidized among the peasantry
The puppet play, his tragic history;
With a white glove he boxed the devil's ears
And with a black his own. Tired of this,
He published penny poems about his sins,
In which he placed the heavy emphasis
On the white glove which, for a penny, wins.

Some time before the hemorrhage of the Kings
Of France, he turned respectable and taught;
Quite suddenly everything that he had thought
Seemed to grow scholars' beards and angels' wings.
It was the Overthrow. On Reason's throne
He sat with the fair Phrygian on his knees
And called all universities his own,
As plausible a figure as you please.

Then back to Germany as the sages' sage
To preach comparative science to the young
Who came from every land in a great throng
And knew they heard the master of the age.
When for a secret formula he paid
The Devil another fragment of his soul,
His scholars wept, and several even prayed
That Satan would restore him to them whole.

Backwardly tolerant, Faustus was expelled
From the Third Reich in Nineteen Thirty-nine.
His exit caused the breaching of the Rhine,
Except for which the frontier might have held.
Five years unknown to enemy and friend
He hid, appearing on the sixth to pose
In an American desert at war's end
Where, at his back, a dome of atoms rose.

In the Waxworks

At midday when the light rebukes the world,
Searching the seams of faces, cracks of walls
And each fault of the beautiful,
Seized by a panic of the street I fled
Into a waxworks where the elite in crime
And great in fame march past in fixed parade.
How pale they were beneath their paint, how pure
The monsters gleaming from the cubicles!

When, as in torsion, I beheld
These malformations of the evil mind
I grew serene and seemed to fall in love,
As one retiring to a moving picture
Or to a gallery of art. I saw
The basest plasm of the human soul
Here turned to sculpture, fingering,
Kissing, and corrupting life.

So back and forth among the leers of wax
I strutted for the idols of the tribe,
Aware that I was on display, not they,
And that I had come down to pray,
As one retires to a synagogue
Or to a plaster saint upon the wall.
Why were these effigies more dear to me
Than haughty mannikins in a window-shop?

I said a rosary for the Presidents
And fell upon my knees before
The Ripper and an exhibit of disease
Revolting more in its soft medium
Than in the flesh. I stroked a prince's hand,
Leaving a thumbprint in the palm. I swore
Allegiance to the suicide whose wrists
Of tallow bled with admirable red.

Why were these images more dear to me
Than faïence dolls or gods of smooth Pentelikon?
Because all statuary turns to death
And only half-art balances.
The fetish lives, idolatry is true,
The crude conception of the putrid face
Sticks to my heart. This criminal in wan
Weak cerement of translucent fat

Is my sweet saint. O heretic, O mute,
When broils efface the Metropolitan
And swinish man from some cloaca creeps
Or that deep midden, his security,
Coming to you in brutish admiration
May he look soft into your eyes;
And you, good wax, may you not then despise
Our sons and daughters, fallen apes.

D. C.

The bad breed of the natives with their hates
That border on a Georgian night,
The short vocabulary, the southern look
That writes a volume on your past, the men
Freeholders of the city-state, the women
Polite for murder—these happen to be;
The rest arrive and never quite remain.

The rest live with an easy homelessness
And common tastelessness, their souls
Weakly lit up by blazing screens and tales
Told by a newspaper. Holidays the vast
Basilicas of the railroad swallow up
Hundreds of thousands, struggling in the tide
For home, the one identity and past.

The noble riches keep themselves, the miles
Of marble breast the empty wind,
The halls of books and pictures manufacture
Their deep patinas, the fountains coldly splash
To the lone sailor, the boulevards stretch out
Farther than Arlington, where all night long
One living soldier marches for the dead.

Only the very foreign, the very proud,
The richest and the very poor
Hid in their creepy purlieus white or black
Adore this whole Augustan spectacle,
And chancelleries perceive the porch of might
Surmounted by the dome in which there lies
No Bonaparte, no Lenin, but a floor.

Yet those who govern live in quaintness, close
In the Georgian ghetto of the best;
What was the simplest of the old becomes
The exquisite palate of the new. Their names
Are admirals and paternalists, their ways
The ways of Lee who, having lost the slaves,
Died farther south, a general in the wrong.

The Convert

Deep in the shadowy bethel of the tired mind,
Where spooks and death lights ride, and Marys, too,
Materialize like senseless ectoplasm
Smiling in blue, out of the blue,
Quite gradually, on a common afternoon,
With no more inner fanfare than a sigh,
With no cross in the air, drizzle of blood,
Beauty of blinding voices from up high,
The man surrenders reason to the ghost
And enters church, via the vestry room.

The groan of positive science, hiss of friends,
Substantiate what doctors call
His rather shameful and benign disease,
But ecumenical heaven clearly sees
His love, his possibilities.
O victory of the Unintelligence,
What mystic rose developing from rock
Is more a miracle than this overthrow?
What Constitution ever promised more
Than his declared insanity?

Yet he shall be less perfect than before,
Being no longer neutral to the Book
But answerable. What formerly were poems,
Precepts, and commonplaces now are laws,
Dantean atlases, and official news.
The dust of ages settles on his mind
And in his ears he hears the click of beads
Adding, adding, adding like a prayer machine
His heartfelt sums. Upon his new-found knees
He treasures up the gold of never-ending day.

All arguments are vain—that Notre Dame
Has plumbing, Baptists shoot their fellowmen,
Hindus are pious, nuns have Cadillacs.
Apologetics anger him who is
The living proof of what he newly knows;
And proudly sorrowing for those who fail
To read his simple summa theologica,
He prays that in the burning they be spared,
And prays for mercy as the south wind blows,
And for all final sins that tip the scale.

Peace on a hundred thousand temples falls
With gently even light, revealing some
With wounded walls and missing faces, some
Spared by the bombardier, and some by God.
In mournful happiness the clerics move
To put the altars back, and the new man,
Heartbroken, walks among the broken saints,
Thinking how heavy is the hand that hates,
How light and secret is the sign of love
In the hour of many significant conversions.

Boy-Man

England's lads are miniature men
To start with, grammar in their shiny hats,
And serious: in America who knows when
Manhood begins? Presidents dance and hug
And while the kind King waves and gravely chats
America wets on England's old green rug.

The boy-man roars. Worry alone will give
This one the verisimilitude of age.
Those white teeth are his own, for he must live
Longer, grow taller than the Texas race.
Fresh are his eyes, his darkening skin the gauge
Of bloods that freely mix beneath his face.

He knows the application of the book
But not who wrote it; shuts it like a shot.
Rather than read he thinks that he will look,
Rather than look he thinks that he will talk,
Rather than talk he thinks that he will not
Bother at all; would rather ride than walk.

His means of conversation is the joke,
Humor his language underneath which lies
The undecoded dialect of the folk.
Abroad he scorns the foreigner: what's old
Is worn, what's different bad, what's odd unwise.
He gives off heat and is enraged by cold.

Charming, becoming to the suits he wears,
The boy-man, younger than his eldest son,
Inherits the state; upon his silver hairs
Time like a panama hat sits at a tilt
And smiles. To him the world has just begun
And every city waiting to be built.

Mister, remove your shoulder from the wheel
And say this prayer, "Increase my vitamins,
Make my decisions of the finest steel,
Pour motor oil upon my troubled spawn,
Forgive the Europeans for their sins,
Establish them, that values may go on."

The Voyage

The ship of my body has danced in the dance of the storm
And pierced to the center the heavy embrace of the tide;
It has plunged to the bottomless trough with the knife of its
    form
And leapt with the prow of its motion elate from the bride.

And now in the dawn I am salt with the taste of the wave,
Which lies with itself and suspires, her beauty asleep,
And I peer at the fishes with jaws that devour and rave
And hunt in her dream for the wrack of our hands in the deep.

But the wind is the odor of love that awakes in the sun
The stream of our voyage that lies on the belt of the seas,
And I gather and breathe in the rays of the darkness undone,
And drift in her silence of morning and sail at my ease,

Where the sponges and rubbery seaweeds and flowers of hair
Uprooted abound in the water and choke in the air.

The New Ring

The new ring oppresses the finger, embarrasses the hand, encumbers the whole arm. The free hand moves to cover the new ring, except late-at-night when the mouth reaches to kiss the soft silver, a sudden thought.

In the lodge of marriage, the secret society of love, the perfect circle binds and separates, moves and is stationary.

Till the ring becomes the flesh, leaving a white trench, and the finger is immune. For the brand is assumed. Till the flesh of the encumbered hand grows over the ring, as living wood over and around the iron spike. Till the value of the reason of the gift is coinworn, and the wound heals.

And until the wound heals, the new ring is a new nail driven through the hand upon the living wood, and the body hangs from the nail, and the nail holds.

The Southerner

He entered with the authority of politeness
And the jokes died in the air. A well-made blaze
Grew round the main log in the fireplace
Spontaneously. I watched its brightness
Spread to the altered faces of my guests.
They did not like the Southerner. I did.
A liberal felt that someone should forbid
That soft voice making its soft arrests.

As when a Negro or a prince extends
His hand to an average man, and the mind
Speeds up a minute and then drops behind,
So did the conversation of my friends.
I was amused by this respectful awe
Which those hotly deny who have no prince.
I watched the frown, the stare, and the wince
Recede into attention, the arms thaw.

I saw my southern evil memories
Raped from my mind before my eyes, my youth
Practicing caste, perfecting the untruth
Of staking honor on the wish to please.
I saw my honor's paradox:
Grandpa, the saintly Jew, keeping his beard
In difficult Virginia, yet endeared
Of blacks and farmers, although orthodox.

The nonsense of the gracious lawn,
The fall of hollow columns in the pines,
Do these deceive more than the rusted signs
Of Jesus on the road? Can they go on
In the timeless manner of all gentlefolk
There in a culture rotted and unweeded
Where the black yoni of the South is seeded
By crooked men in denims thin as silk?

They do go on, denying still the fall
Of Richmond and man, who gently live
On the street above the violence, fugitive,
Graceful, and darling, who recall
The heartbroken country once about to flower,
Full of black poison, beautiful to smell,
Who know how to conform, how to compel,
And how from the best bush to receive a flower.

Recapitulations

I

I was born downtown on a wintry day
    And under the roof where Poe expired;
Tended by nuns my mother lay
    Dark-haired and beautiful and tired.

Doctors and cousins paid their call,
    The rabbi and my father helped.
A crucifix burned on the wall
    Of the bright room where I was whelped.

At one week all my family prayed,
    Stuffed wine and cotton in my craw;
The rabbi blessed me with a blade
    According to the Mosaic Law.

The white steps blazed in Baltimore
    And cannas and white statuary.
I went home voluble and sore
    Influenced by Abraham and Mary.

II

At one the Apocalypse had spoken,
Von Moltke fell, I was housebroken.

At two how could I understand
The murder of Archduke Ferdinand?

France was involved with history,
I with my thumbs when I was three.

A sister came, we neared a war,
Paris was shelled when I was four.

I joined in our peach-kernel drive
For poison gas when I was five.

At six I cheered the big parade,
Burned sparklers and drank lemonade.

At seven I passed at school though I
Was far too young to say *Versailles*.

At eight the boom began to tire,
I tried to set our house on fire.

The Bolsheviks had drawn the line,
Lenin was stricken, I was nine.

—What evils do not retrograde
To my first odious decade?

III

Saints by whose pages I would swear,
    My Zarathustra, Edward Lear,
Ulysses, Werther, fierce Flaubert,
    Where are my books of yesteryear?

Sixteen and sixty are a pair;
    We twice live by philosophies;
My marginalia of the hair,
    Are you at one with Socrates?

Thirty subsides yet does not dare,
    Sixteen and sixty bang their fists.
How is it that I no longer care
    For Kant and the Transcendentalists?

Public libraries lead to prayer,
    EN ΑΡΧΗ ἦν ὁ λόγος—still
Eliot and John are always there
    To tempt our admirari nil.

IV

I lived in a house of panels,
    Victorian, darkly made;
A virgin in bronze and marble
    Leered from the balustrade.

The street was a tomb of virtues,
    Autumnal for dreams and haunts;
I gazed from the polished windows
    Toward a neighborhood of aunts.

Mornings I practiced piano,
    Wrote elegies and sighed;
The evenings were conversations
    Of poetry and suicide.

Weltschmerz and mysticism,
    What tortures we undergo!
I loved with the love of Heinrich
    And the poison of Edgar Poe.

V

My first small book was nourished in the dark,
Secretly written, published, and inscribed.
Bound in wine-red, it made no brilliant mark.
Rather impossible relatives subscribed.

The best review was one I wrote myself
Under the name of a then-dearest friend.
Two hundred volumes stood upon my shelf
Saying my golden name from end to end.

I was not proud but seriously stirred;
Sorrow was song and money poetry's maid!
Sorrow I had in many a ponderous word,
But were the piper and the printer paid?

VI

The third-floor thoughts of discontented youth
Once saw the city, hardened against truth,
Get set for war. He coupled a last rime
And waited for the summons to end time.

It came. The box-like porch where he had sat,
The four bright boxes of a medium flat,
Chair he had sat in, glider where he lay
Reading the poets and prophets of his day,

He assigned abstractly to his dearest friend,
Glanced at the little street hooked at the end,
The line of poplars lately touched with spring,
Lovely as Laura, breathless, beckoning.

Mother was calm, until he left the door;
The trolley passed his sweetheart's house before
She was awake. The Armory was cold,
But naked, shivering, shocked he was enrolled.

It was the death he never quite forgot
Through the four years of death, and like as not
The true death of the best of all of us
Whose present life is largely posthumous.

VII

We waged a war within a war,
     A cause within a cause;
The glory of it was withheld
     In keeping with the laws
Whereby the public need not know
The pitfalls of the status quo.

Love was the reason for the blood:
     The black men of our land
Were seen to walk with pure white girls
     Laughing and hand in hand.

This most unreasonable state
No feeling White would tolerate.

We threw each other from the trams,
    We carried knives and pipes,
We sacrificed in self-defense
    Some of the baser types,
But though a certain number died
You would not call it fratricide.

The women with indignant tears
    Professed to love the Blacks,
And dark and wooly heads still met
    With heads of English flax.
Only the cockney could conceive
Of any marriage so naïve.

Yet scarcely fifty years before
    Their fathers rode to shoot
The undressed aborigines,
    Though not to persecute.
A fine distinction lies in that
They have no others to combat.

By order of the high command
    The black men were removed
To the interior and north;
    The crisis thus improved,
Even the women could detect
Their awful fall from intellect.

VIII

I plucked the bougainvillaea
    In Queensland in time of war;
The train stopped at the station
    And I reached it from my door.

I have never kept a flower
  And this one I never shall
I thought as I laid the blossom
  In the leaves of *Les Fleurs du Mal.*

I read my book in the desert
  In the time of death and fear,
The flower slipped from the pages
  And fell to my lap, my dear.

I sent it inside my letter,
  The purplest kiss I knew,
And thus you abused my passion
  With "A most Victorian Jew."

from Poems 1940-1953

Adam and Eve

I   The Sickness of Adam

In the beginning, at every step, he turned
As if by instinct to the East to praise
The nature of things. Now every path was learned
He lost the lifted, almost flower-like gaze

Of a temple dancer. He began to walk
Slowly, like one accustomed to be alone.
He found himself lost in the field of talk;
Thinking became a garden of its own.

In it were new things: words he had never said,
Beasts he had never seen and knew were not
In the true garden, terrors, and tears shed
Under a tree by him, for some new thought.

And the first anger. Once he flung a staff
At softly coupling sheep and struck the ram.
It broke away. And God heard Adam laugh
And for his laughter made the creature lame.

And wanderlust. He stood upon the Wall
To search the unfinished countries lying wide
And waste, where not a living thing could crawl,
And yet he would descend, as if to hide.

His thought drew down the guardian at the gate,
To whom man said, "What danger am I in?"
And the angel, hurt in spirit, seemed to hate
The wingless thing that worried after sin,

For it said nothing but marvelously unfurled
Its wings and arched them shimmering overhead,
Which must have been the signal from the world
That the first season of our life was dead.

Adam fell down with labor in his bones,
And God approached him in the cool of day
And said, "This sickness in your skeleton
Is longing. I will remove it from your clay."

He said also, "I made you strike the sheep."
It began to rain and God sat down beside
The sinking man. When he was fast asleep
He wet his right hand deep in Adam's side

And drew the graceful rib out of his breast.
Far off, the latent streams began to flow
And birds flew out of Paradise to nest
On earth. Sadly the angel watched them go.

II The Recognition of Eve

Whatever it was she had so fiercely fought
Had fled back to the sky, but still she lay
With arms outspread, awaiting its assault,
Staring up through the branches of the tree,
The fig tree. Then she drew a shuddering breath
And turned her head instinctively his way.
She had fought birth as dying men fight death.

Her sigh awakened him. He turned and saw
A body swollen, as though formed of fruits,
White as the flesh of fishes, soft and raw.
He hoped she was another of the brutes
So he crawled over and looked into her eyes,
The human wells that pool all absolutes.
It was like looking into double skies.

And when she spoke the first word (it was *thou*)
He was terror-stricken, but she raised her hand
And touched his wound where it was fading now,
For he must feel the place to understand.
Then he recalled the longing that had torn
His side, and while he watched it whitely mend,
He felt it stab him suddenly like a thorn.

He thought the woman had hurt him. Was it she
Or the same sickness seeking to return;
Or was there any difference, the pain set free
And she who seized him now as hard as iron?
Her fingers bit his body. She looked old
And involuted, like the newly-born.
He let her hurt him till she loosed her hold.

Then she forgot him and she wearily stood
And went in search of water through the grove.
Adam could see her wandering through the wood,
Studying her footsteps as her body wove
In light and out of light. She found a pool
And there he followed shyly to observe.
She was already turning beautiful.

III The Kiss

The first kiss was with stumbling fingertips.
Their bodies grazed each other as if by chance
And touched and untouched in a kind of dance.
Second, they found out touching with their lips.

Some obscure angel, pausing on his course,
Shed such a brightness on the face of Eve
That Adam in grief was ready to believe
He had lost her love. The third kiss was by force.

Their lips formed foreign, unimagined oaths
When speaking of the Tree of Guilt. So wide
Their mouths, they drank each other from inside.
A gland of honey burst within their throats.

But something rustling hideously overhead,
They jumped up from the fourth caress and hid.

IV The Tree of Guilt

Why, on her way to the oracle of Love,
Did she not even glance up at the Tree
Of Life, that giant with the whitish cast
And glinting leaves and berries of dull gray,
As though covered with mold? But who would taste
The medicine of immortality,
And who would "be as God"? And in what way?

So she came breathless to the lowlier one
And like a priestess of the cult she knelt,
Holding her breasts in token for a sign,
And prayed the spirit of the burdened bough
That the great power of the tree be seen
And lift itself out of the Tree of Guilt
Where it had hidden in the leaves till now.

Or did she know already? Had the peacock
Rattling its quills, glancing its thousand eyes
At her, the iridescence of the dove,
Stench of the he-goat, everything that joins
Told her the mystery? It was not enough,
So from the tree the snake began to rise
And dropt its head and pointed at her loins.

She fell and hid her face and still she saw
The spirit of the tree emerge and slip
Into the open sky until it stood
Straight as a standing-stone, and spilled its seed.
And all the seed were serpents of the good.
Again the snake was seized and from its lip
It spat the venomous evil of the deed.

And it was over. But the woman lay
Stricken with what she knew, ripe in her thought
Like a fresh apple fallen from the limb
And rotten, like a fruit that lies too long.
This way she rose, ripe-rotten in her prime
And spurned the cold thing coiled against her foot
And called her husband, in a kind of song.

V The Confession

As on the first day her first word was *thou*.
He waited while she said, "Thou art the tree."
And while she said, almost accusingly,
Looking at nothing, "Thou art the fruit I took."
She seemed smaller by inches as she spoke,
And Adam wondering touched her hair and shook,
Half understanding. He answered softly, "How?"

And for the third time, in the third way, Eve:
"The tree that rises from the middle part
Of the garden." And almost tenderly, "Thou art
The garden. *We*." Then she was overcome,
And Adam coldly, lest he should succumb
To pity, standing at the edge of doom,
Comforted her like one about to leave.

She sensed departure and she stood aside
Smiling and bitter. But he asked again,
"How did you eat? With what thing did you sin?"
And Eve with body slackened and uncouth,
"Under the tree I took the fruit of truth
From an angel. I ate it with my other mouth."
And saying so, she did not know she lied.

It was the man who suddenly released
From doubt, wept in the woman's heavy arms,
Those double serpents, subtly winding forms
That climb and drop about the manly boughs,
And dry with weeping, fiery and aroused,
Fell on her face to slake his terrible thirst
And bore her body earthward like a beast.

VI Shame

The hard blood falls back in the manly fount,
The soft door closes under Venus' mount,
The ovoid moon moves to the Garden's side
And dawn comes, but the lovers have not died.
They have not died but they have fallen apart
In sleep, like equal halves of the same heart.

How to teach shame? How to teach nakedness
To the already naked? How to express
Nudity? How to open innocent eyes
And separate the innocent from the wise?
And how to re-establish the guilty tree
In infinite gardens of humanity?

By marring the image, by the black device
Of the goat-god, by the clown of Paradise,
By fruits of cloth and by the navel's bud,
By itching tendrils and by strings of blood,
By ugliness, by the shadow of our fear,
By ridicule, by the fig-leaf patch of hair.

Whiter than tombs, whiter than whitest clay,
Exposed beneath the whitening eye of day,
They awoke and saw the covering that reveals.
They thought they were changing into animals.
Like animals they bellowed terrible cries
And clutched each other, hiding each other's eyes.

VII Exile

The one who gave the warning with his wings,
Still doubting them, held out the sword of flame
Against the Tree of Whiteness as they came
Angrily, slowly by, like exiled kings,

And watched them at the broken-open gate
Stare in the distance long and overlong,
And then, like peasants, pitiful and strong,
Take the first step toward earth and hesitate.

For Adam raised his head and called aloud,
"My Father, who has made the garden pall,
Giving me all things and then taking all,
Who with your opposite nature has endowed

Woman, give us your hand for our descent.
Needing us greatly, even in our disgrace,
Guide us, for gladly do we leave this place
For our own land and wished-for banishment."

But woman prayed, "Guide us to Paradise."
Around them slunk the uneasy animals,
Strangely excited, uttering coughs and growls,
And bounded down into the wild abyss.

And overhead the last migrating birds,
Then empty sky. And when the two had gone
A slow half-dozen steps across the stone,
The angel came and stood among the shards

And called them, as though joyously, by name.
They turned in dark amazement and beheld
Eden ablaze with fires of red and gold,
The garden dressed for dying in cold flame,

And it was autumn, and the present world.

The Tingling Back

Sometimes deeply immured in white-washed tower
    quiet at ink and thinking book,
        alone with my own smoke,
the blood at rest, the body far below,
    swiftly there falls an angry shower
        of arrows upon my back,
like bees or electric needles run amok
    between my flesh and shirt. I know
        then I have touched the pain
of amour-propre, of something yesterday
    I said and I should not have said,
        I did and must not do.
These needles wing their insights from my brain
    and through and through my flesh they play
        to prick my skin with red
letters of shame and blue blurs of tattoo.
    I sweat and take my medicine
        for one must be sincere
and study one's sincerity like a crime:
    to be the very last to smile,
        the first one to begin
(when danger streaks the atmosphere) to fear,
    to pocket praises like a dime,
        to pet the crocodile,
to see a foreign agony as stone,
    to ravel dreams in crowded room,
        to let the hair grow tall,
to skin the eye and thrust it to the wind.
    Yet if I stood with God alone
        inside the blinding tomb
I would not feel embarrassment at all
    nor those hot needles of the mind
        which are so clean. I'd ask
not if I'd known the tissue of my will

and scarified my body white,
            but whether, insincere,
I'd grown to the simplicity of a mask;
        and if in natural error still
                whether my fingers might
destroy the true and keep the error near.

The Minute

The office building treads the marble dark,
The mother-clock with wide and golden dial
Suffers and glows. Now is the hour of birth
Of the tremulous egg. Now is the time of correction.
O midnight, zero of eternity,
Soon on a million bureaus of the city
Will lie the new-born minute.

The new-born minute on the bureau lies,
Scratching the glass with infant kick, cutting
With diamond cry the crystal and expanse
Of timelessness. This pretty tick of death
Etches its name upon the air. I turn
Titanically in distant sleep, expelling
From my lungs the bitter gas of life.

The loathsome minute grows in length and strength,
Bending its spring to forge an iron hour
That rusts from link to link, the last one bright,
The late one dead. Between the shining works
Range the clean angels, studying that tick
Like a strange dirt, but will not pick it up
Nor move it gingerly out of harm's way.

An angel is stabbed and is carried aloft howling,
For devils have gathered on a ruby jewel
Like red mites on a berry; others arrive
To tend the points with oil and smooth the heat.
See how their vicious faces, lit with sweat,
Worship the train of wheels; see how they pull
The tape-worm Time from nothing into thing.

I with my distant heart lie wide awake
Smiling at that Swiss-perfect engine room
Driven by tiny evils. Knowing no harm
Even of gongs that loom and move in towers
And hands as high as iron masts, I sleep,
At which sad sign the angels in a flock
Rise and sweep past me, spinning threads of fear.

Love for a Hand

Two hands lie still, the hairy and the white,
And soon down ladders of reflected light
The sleepers climb in silence. Gradually
They separate on paths of long ago,
Each winding on his arm the unpleasant clew
That leads, live as a nerve, to memory.

But often when too steep her dream descends,
Perhaps to the grotto where her father bends
To pick her up, the husband wakes as though
He had forgotten something in the house.
Motionless he eyes the room that glows
With the little animals of light that prowl

This way and that. Soft are the beasts of light
But softer still her hand that drifts so white
Upon the whiteness. How like a water-plant
It floats upon the black canal of sleep,
Suspended upward from the distant deep
In pure achievement of its lovely want!

Quietly then he plucks it and it folds
And is again a hand, small as a child's.
He would revive it but it barely stirs
And so he carries it off a little way
And breaks it open gently. Now he can see
The sweetness of the fruit, his hand eats hers.

Israel

When I think of the liberation of Palestine,
When my eye conceives the great black English line
Spanning the world news of two thousand years,
My heart leaps forward like a hungry dog,
My heart is thrown back on its tangled chain,
My soul is hangdog in a Western chair.

When I think of the battle for Zion I hear
The drop of chains, the starting forth of feet
And I remain chained in a Western chair.
My blood beats like a bird against a wall,
I feel the weight of prisons in my skull
Falling away; my forebears stare through stone.

When I see the name of Israel high in print
The fences crumble in my flesh; I sink
Deep in a Western chair and rest my soul.
I look the stranger clear to the blue depths
Of his unclouded eye. I say my name
Aloud for the first time unconsciously.

Speak of the tillage of a million heads
No more. Speak of the evil myth no more
Of one who harried Jesus on his way
Saying, *Go faster*. Speak no more
Of the yellow badge, *secta nefaria*.
Speak the name only of the living land.

Glass Poem

The afternoon lies glazed upon the wall
And on the window shines the scene-like bay,
And on the dark reflective floor a ray
Falls, and my thoughts like ashes softly fall.

And I look up as one who looks through glass
And sees the thing his soul clearly desires,
Who stares until his vision flags and tires,
But from whose eye the image fails to pass;

Until a wish crashes the vitreous air
And comes to your real hands across this space,
Thief-like and deeply cut to touch your face,
Dearly, most bitterly to touch your hair.

And I could shatter these transparent lights,
Could thrust my arms and bring your body through,
Break from the subtle spectrum the last hue
And change my eyes to dark soft-seeing nights.

But the sun stands and the hours stare like brass
And day flows thickly into permanent time,
And toward your eyes my threatening wishes climb
Where you move through a sea of solid glass.

The Figurehead

Watching my paralytic friend
Caught in the giant clam of himself
Fast on the treacherous shoals of his bed,
I look away to the place he had left
Where at a decade's distance he appeared
To pause in his walk and think of a limp.
One day he arrived at the street bearing
The news that he dragged an ancient foot:
The people on their porches seemed to sway.

Though there are many wired together
In this world and the next, my friend
Strains in his clamps. He is all sprung
And locked in the rust of inner change.
The therapist who plucks him like a harp
Is a cold torture: the animal bleats
And whimpers on its far seashore
As she leans to her find with a smooth hunger.

Somewhere in a storm my pity went down:
It was a wooden figurehead
With sea-hard breasts and polished mouth.
But women wash my friend with brine
From shallow inlets of their eyes,
And women rock my friend with waves
That pulsate from the female moon.
They gather at his very edge and haul
My driftwood friend toward their fires.

Speaking of dancing, joking of sex,
I watch my paralytic friend
And seek my pity in those wastes where he
Becomes my bobbing figurehead.
Then as I take my leave I wade
Loudly into the shallows of his pain,
I splash like a vacationer,
I scare his legs and stir the time of day
With rosy clouds of sediment.

F. O. Matthiessen: An Anniversary

To learn the meaning of his leap to death
What need to know the wounds he carried down
To his crushing sleep? For the shocked town,
Bombed by his suicide, the ejaculation of blood,
Summarized it neatly in the shibboleth
Of mutual forgiveness: Matthiessen was good.

Yet there remained a reminder on the stair
Of nothing: high on the ledge of that hotel
Where an unbalanced soldier heard the yell
Of the depraved unchristian mob to leap,
But could not, being imperfect in despair,
Jump at their will into a hell so deep,

And fell back finally in the waiting arms
Of a traffic cop, a blond girl, and a priest.
And thus the loud and thousand-handed beast
Melted away.—What mob did Matthiessen
Hear chanting in rhythm, and what uniforms
Tried to retrieve him to the world of men?

What was he saying in his heavy fall
Through space, so broken by the hand of stone?
What word was that stopped like a telephone
Torn with its nervous wire from the wall?
Does not the condemned man raise his voice to call
His phrase of justice down the empty hall?

And who betrayed him finally. Was it I?
Some poet who turned his praises into blame,
Or some historian of the parlor game
Of war? Or the easy capture of the schloss
By Slavs? The Americanization of the spy?
The death of a friend? Was there no further loss?

Left with no ground except the ground that kills,
He mourned the death of politics and died.
It was, as it were, a statesman's suicide,
For when out of the window he had flung
His life upon those uncharitable hills,
Did he not will his charity to the young?

Ego

Ego is not persona: in childhood
He rules the little senses, plays at eyes,
Betters the nose, learns warm and soft and cold,
Reacts but cannot act. Ego is old:
He fights but neither laughs nor cries,
Stares but is neither bad nor good.

Ego is not narcissus: if in youth
He lingers at the mirror, he is clear,
Is not in love and never seeks a friend,
Makes all dependent yet does not depend,
Inspects, indulges, does not fear,
Remembers all. Ego is truth.

Ego does not desire or acquire,
Is not the mouth and not the reaching hand,
Dreams never, sleeps at bedtime, rises first,
Sees that the hell of darkness is dispersed,
Is pale in winter, in summer tanned,
Functions alike in ice and fire.

Ego domesticated serves the man
But is no servant, stands aside for will,
Gives no advice, takes none. Ego can fail;
Pampered he softens, struck withdraws like snail.
Trust him to know and to keep still,
Love him as much as brother can.

A Calder

To raise an iron tree
Is a wooden irony,
But to cause it to sail
In a clean perpetual way
Is to play
Upon the spaces of the scale.
Climbing the stairs we say,
Is it work or is it play?

Alexander Calder made it
Work and play:
Leaves that will never burn
But were fired to be born,
Twigs that are stiff with life
And bend as to the magnet's breath,
Each segment back to back,
The whole a hanging burst of flak.

Still the base metals,
Touched by autumnal paint
Fall through no autumn
But, turning, feint
In a fall beyond trees,
Where forests are not wooded,
There is no killing breeze,
And iron is blooded.

Carte Postale

It is so difficult not to go with it
Once it is seen. It tears the mind agape
With butcher force, with intellectual rape,
And the body hangs by a hair above the pit.

In whose brain, when the order was destroyed,
Did it take form and pose, and when the eye
Clicked, was he guillotined into the void
Where the vile emulsion hangs in strips to dry?

It rose with obvious relish to be viewed,
And lay at a sewer's mouth in the grainy dawn
Where a cop found it. It seemed a platitude
Like a bad postcard of the Parthenon.

I know its family tree, its dossier,
Its memory older than Pompeian walls.
Not that it lives but that it looks at day
Shocks. In the night, wherever it is, it calls,

And never fades, but lies flat and uncurled
Even in blast furnace at the fire's core,
Feeding fat tallow to our sunken world
Deep in the riches of our father's drawer.

The Phenomenon

How lovely it was, after the official fright,
To walk in the shadowy drifts, as if the clouds
Saturated with the obscurity of night
Had died and fallen piecemeal into shrouds.

What crepes there were, what sables heaped on stones,
What soft shakos on posts, tragically gay!
And oil-pool flooded fields that blackly shone
The more black under the liquid eye of day!

It was almost warmer to the touch than sands
And sweeter-tasting than the white, and yet
Walking, the children held their fathers' hands
Like visitors to a mine or parapet.

Then black it snowed again and while it fell
You could see the sun, an irritated rim
Wheeling through smoke; each from his shallow hell
Experienced injured vision growing dim.

But one day all was clear, and one day soon,
Sooner than those who witnessed it had died,
Nature herself forgot the phenomenon,
Her faulty snowfall brilliantly denied.

The Potomac

The thin Potomac scarcely moves
But to divide Virginia from today;
   Rider, whichever is your way
You go due south and neither South improves;
Not this, of fractured columns and queer rents
   And rags that charm the nationalist,
Not that, the axle of the continents,
Nor the thin sky that flows unprejudiced
This side and that, cleansing the poisoned breath.

For Thomas died a Georgian death
And now the legion bones of Arlington
   Laid out in marble alphabets
Stare on the great tombs of the capitol
   Where heroes calcified and cool
   Ponder the soldier named Unknown
Whose lips are guarded with live bayonets.

Yet he shall speak though sentries walk
And columns with their cold Corinthian stalk
   Shed gold-dust pollen on Brazil
   To turn the world to Roman chalk;
Yet he shall speak, yet he shall speak
   Whose sulphur lit the flood-lit Dome,
   Whose hands were never in the kill,
Whose will was furrows of Virginia loam.

But not like London blown apart by boys
Who learned the books of love in English schools,
His name shall strike the fluted columns down;
These shall lie buried deep as fifty Troys,
The money fade like leaves from green to brown,
And embassies dissolve to molecules.

Going to School

What shall I teach in the vivid afternoon
With the sun warming the blackboard and a slip
Of cloud catching my eye?
Only the cones and sections of the moon
Out of some flaking page of scholarship,
Only some foolish heresy
To counteract the authority of prose.
The ink runs freely and the dry chalk flows
Into the silent night of seven slates
Where I create the universe as if
It grew out of some old rabbinic glyph
Or hung upon the necessity of Yeats.

O dry imaginations, drink this dust
That grays the room and powders my coat sleeve,
For in this shaft of light
I dance upon the intellectual crust
Of our own age and hold this make-believe
Like holy-work before your sight.
This is the list of books that time has burned,
These are the lines that only poets have learned,
The frame of dreams, the symbols that dilate;
Yet when I turn from this dark exercise
I meet your bright and world-considering eyes
That build and build and never can create.

I gaze down on the garden with its green
Axial lines and scientific pond
And watch a man in white
Stiffly pursue a butterfly between
Square hedges where he takes it overhand
Into the pocket of his net.
Ah psyche, sinking in the bottled fumes,
Dragging your slow wings while the hunt resumes.

I say, "He placed an image on the pool
Of the Great Mind to float there like a leaf
And then sink downward to the dark belief
Of the Great Memory of the Hermetic School."

I say, "Linnaeus drowned the names of flowers
With the black garlands of his Latin words;
The gardens now are his,
The drug-bright blossoms of the glass are ours.
I think a million taxidermist's birds
Sing in the mind of Agassiz
Who still retained one image of the good,
Who said a fish is but a thought of God.
—This is the flat world circled by its dogs,
This is the right triangle held divine
Before bald Euclid drew his empty line
And shame fell on the ancient astrologues."

The eyes strike angles on the farther wall,
Divine geometry forms upon the page,
I feel a sense of shame.
Then as the great design begins to pall
A cock crows in a laboratory cage
And I proceed. "As for the name,
It is the potency itself of thing,
It is the power-of-rising of the wing;
Without it death and feathers, for neither reed
Of Solomon nor quill of Shakespeare's goose
Ever did more or less than to deduce
Letter from number in our ignorant creed."

And what if he who blessed these walls should walk
Invisibly in the room?—My conscience prates,
"The great biologist
Who read the universe in a piece of chalk
Said all knowledge is good, all learning waits,
And wrong hypotheses exist
To order knowledge and to set it right.

We burn, he said, that others may have light.
These are the penetralia of the school
Of the last century. Under a later sky
We call both saint and fool to prophesy
The second cycle brimming at the full."

Then the clock strikes and I erase the board,
Clearing the cosmos with a sweep of felt,
Voiding my mind as well.
Now that the blank of reason is restored
And they go talking of the crazy Celt
And ghosts that sipped his muscatel,
I must escape their laughter unaware
And sidle past the question on the stair
To gain my office. Is the image lost
That burned and shivered in the speculum
Or does it hover in the upper room?
Have I deceived the student or the ghost?

Here in the quiet of the book-built dark
Where masonry of volumes walls me in
I should expect to find,
Returning to me on a lower arc,
Some image bodying itself a skin,
Some object thinking forth a mind.
This search necessitates no closer look.
I close my desk and choose a modern book
And leave the building. Low, as to astound,
The sun stands with its body on the line
That separates us. Low, as to combine,
The sun touches its image to the ground.

The Alphabet

The letters of the Jews as strict as flames
Or little terrible flowers lean
Stubbornly upwards through the perfect ages,
Singing through solid stone the sacred names.
The letters of the Jews are black and clean
And lie in chain-line over Christian pages.
The chosen letters bristle like barbed wire
That hedge the flesh of man,
Twisting and tightening the book that warns.
These words, this burning bush, this flickering pyre
Unsacrifices the bled son of man
Yet plaits his crown of thorns.

Where go the tipsy idols of the Roman
Past synagogues of patient time,
Where go the sisters of the Gothic rose,
Where go the blue eyes of the Polish women
Past the almost natural crime,
Past the still speaking embers of ghettos,
There rise the tinder flowers of the Jews.
The letters of the Jews are dancing knives
That carve the heart of darkness seven ways.
These are the letters that all men refuse
And will refuse until the king arrives
And will refuse until the death of time
And all is rolled back in the book of days.

Messias

Alone in the darkling apartment the boy
Was reading poetry when the doorbell rang;
The sound sped to his ear and winged his joy,
The book leaped from his lap on broken wing.

Down the gilt stairwell then he peered
Where an old man of patriarchal race
Climbed in an eastern language with his beard
A black halo around his paper face.

His glasses spun with vision and his hat
Was thick with fur in the August afternoon;
His silk suit crackled heavily with light
And in his hand a rattling canister shone.

Bigger he grew and softer the root words
Of the hieratic language of his heart,
And faced the boy, who flung the entrance wide
And fled in terror from the nameless hurt.

Past every door like a dead thing he swam,
Past the entablatures of the kitchen walls,
Down the red ringing of the fire escape
Singing with sun, to the green grass he came,

Sickeningly green, leaving the man to lurch
Bewildered through the house and seat himself
In the sacrificial kitchen after his march,
To study the strange boxes on the shelf.

There mother found him mountainous and alone,
Mumbling some singsong in a monotone,
Crumbling breadcrumbs in his scholar's hand
That wanted a donation for the Holy Land.

The Confirmation

When mothers weep and fathers richly proud
Worship on Sunday morning their tall son
And girls in white like angels in a play
    Tiptoe between the potted palms
    And all the crimson windows pray,
        The preacher bound in black
Opens his hands like pages of a book
    And holds the black and crimson law
    For every boy to look.

Last night between the chapters of a dream,
The photograph still sinning in the drawer,
The boy awoke; the moon shone in the yard
    On hairy hollyhocks erect
    And buds of roses pink and hard
        And on the solid wall
A square of light like movies fell to pose
    An actress naked in the night
        As hollyhock and rose.

And to confirm his sex, breathless and white
With benediction self-bestowed he knelt
Oh tightly married to his childish grip,
    And unction smooth as holy-oil
    Fell from the vessel's level lip
        Upon the altar-cloth;
Like Easter boys the blood sang in his head
    And all night long the tallow beads
        Like tears dried in the bed.

Come from the church, you parents and you girls,
And walk with kisses and with happy jokes
Beside this man. Be doubly proud, you priest,
    Once for his passion in the rose,
    Once for his body self-released;
       And speak aloud of her
Who in the perfect consciousness of joy
    Stood naked in the electric light
    And woke the hidden boy.

The Olive Tree

Save for a lusterless honing-stone of moon
The sky stretches its flawless canopy
Blue as the blue silk of the Jewish flag
Over the valley and out to sea.
It is bluest just above the olive tree.
You cannot find in twisted Italy
So straight a one; it stands not on a crag,
Is not humpbacked with bearing in scored stone,
But perfectly erect in my front yard,
Oblivious of its fame. The fruit is hard,
Multitudinous, acid, tight on the stem;
The leaves ride boat-like in the brimming sun,
Going nowhere and scooping up the light.
It is the silver tree, the holy tree,
Tree of all attributes.

     Now on the lawn
The olives fall by thousands, and I delight
To shed my tennis shoes and walk on them,
Pressing them coldly into the deep grass,
In love and reverence for the total loss.

The Jew at Christmas Eve

I see the thin bell-ringer standing at corners
Fine as a breath, in cloth of red,
With eyes afar and long arm of a reed
Weakly waving a religious bell,
Under the boom of caroling hours
I see the thin bell-ringer standing still,
Breasting the prosperous tide on the Christmas pave.

I see the thin bell-ringer repeating himself
From corner to corner, year to year,
Struggling to stand beneath the windy blare
Of horns that carol out of walls.
He would attract a crying waif
Or garrulous old woman down-at-heels
Or a pair of lovers on the icy pave.

Whom do you summon, Santa of the spare?
Whom do you summon, arm of a reed?
Whom do you cheer with ringing and whom chide,
And who stops at the tripod at your side
And wishes you the time of year?
A few who feed the cauldron of the unfed,
The iron cauldron on the fireless pave.

I seen the thin bell-ringer as a flame
Of scarlet, trying to throw the flame
With each sweep of the bell. The tide pours on
And wets the ringer in cloth of red
And parts around the ringer of flame
With eyes afar and long arm of a reed
Who shakes the fire on the snowy pave.

The First Time

Behind shut doors, in shadowy quarantine,
There shines the lamp of iodine and rose
That stains all love with its medicinal bloom.
This boy, who is no more than seventeen,
Not knowing what to do, takes off his clothes
As one might in a doctor's anteroom.

Then in a cross-draft of fear and shame
Feels love hysterically burn away,
A candle swimming down to nothingness
Put out by its own wetted gusts of flame,
And he stands smooth as uncarved ivory
Heavily curved for some expert caress.

And finally sees the always open door
That is invisible till the time has come,
And half falls through as through a rotten wall
To where chairs twist with dragons from the floor
And the great bed drugged with its own perfume
Spreads its carnivorous flower-mouth for all.

The girl is sitting with her back to him;
She wears a black thing and she rakes her hair,
Hauling her round face upward like moonrise;
She is younger than he, her angled arms are slim
And like a country girl her feet are bare.
She watches him behind her with old eyes,

Transfixing him in space like some grotesque,
Far, far from her where he is still alone
And being here is more and more untrue.
Then she turns round, as one turns at a desk,
And looks at him, too naked and too soon,
And almost gently asks: *Are you a Jew?*

Teasing the Nuns

Up in the elevator went the nuns
    Wild as a cage of undomestic ducks,
Turning and twittering their unclippped hats,
    Gay in captivity, a flirtatious flock
Of waterfowl tipped with black
    Above the traffic and its searing suns.
Higher and higher in the wall we flew
    Hauled on by rosaries and split strands of hair,
Myself in the center sailing like Sinbad
    Yanked into heaven by a hairy Roc;
Whence we emerged into a towery cell
    Where holy cross was splayed upon the wall
In taxidermy of the eternal. They
    Bedecked in elegant bird-names dropped
Curtsies, I thought, and merrily sat
    And fixed their gaze on mine that floated out
Between them and their poised hawk.

"Sisters," I said.—And then I stopped.

The Murder of Moses

By reason of despair we set forth behind you
And followed the pillar of fire like a doubt,
To hold to belief wanted a sign,
Called the miracle of the staff and the plagues
Natural phenomena.

We questioned the expediency of the march,
Gossiped about you. What was escape
To the fear of going forward and Pharaoh's wheels?
When the chariots mired and the army flooded
Our cry of horror was one with theirs.

You always went alone, a little ahead,
Prophecy disturbed you, you were not a fanatic.
The women said you were meek, the men
Regarded you as a typical leader.
You and your black wife might have been foreigners.

We even discussed your parentage; were you really a Jew?
We remembered how Joseph had made himself a prince,
All of us shared in the recognition
Of his skill of management, sense of propriety,
Devotion to his brothers and Israel.

We hated you daily. Our children died. The water spilled.
It was as if you were trying to lose us one by one.
Our wandering seemed the wandering of your mind,
The cloud believed we were tireless,
We expressed our contempt and our boredom openly.

At last you ascended the rock; at last returned.
Your anger that day was probably His.

When we saw you come down from the mountain, your skin
      alight
And the stones of our law flashing,
We fled like animals and the dancers scattered.

We watched where you overturned the calf on the fire,
We hid when you broke the tablets on the rock,
We wept when we drank the mixture of gold and water.
We had hoped you were lost or had left us.
This was the day of our greatest defilement.

You were simple of heart; you were sorry for Miriam,
You reasoned with Aaron, who was your enemy.
However often you cheered us with songs and prayers
We cursed you again. The serpent bit us,
And mouth to mouth you entreated the Lord for our sake.

At the end of it all we gave you the gift of death.
Invasion and generalship were spared you.
The hand of our direction, resignedly you fell,
And while officers prepared for the river-crossing
The One God blessed you and covered you with earth.

Though you were mortal and once committed murder
You assumed the burden of the covenant,
Spoke for the world and for our understanding.
Converse with God made you a thinker,
Taught us all early justice, made us a race.

The Crucifix in the Filing Cabinet

Out of the filing cabinet of true steel
That saves from fire my rags of letters, bills,
Manuscripts, contracts, all the trash of praise
Which one acquires to prove and prove his days;

Out of the drawer that rolls on hidden wheels
I drew a crucifix with beaded chain,
Still new and frightened-looking and absurd.
I picked it up as one picks up a bird

And placed it on my palm. It formed a pile
Like a small mound of stones on which there stands
A tree crazy with age, and on the tree
Some ancient teacher hanging by his hands.

I found a velvet bag sewn by the Jews
For holy shawls and frontlets and soft thongs
That bind the arm at morning for great wrongs
Done in a Pharaoh's time. The crucifix

I dropped down in the darkness of this pouch,
Thought tangled with thought and chain with chain,
Till time untie the dark with greedy look,
Crumble the cross and bleed the leathery vein.

from The Bourgeois Poet

The world is my dream, says the wise child...

The world is my dream, says the wise child, ever so wise, not
    stepping on lines. I am the world, says the wise-eyed
    child. I made you, mother. I made you, sky. Take care
    or I'll put you back in my dream.

If I look at the sun the sun will explode, says the wicked boy.
    If I look at the moon I'll drain away. Where I stay I
    hold them in their places. Don't ask me what I'm doing.

The simple son was sent to science college. There he learned
    how everything worked.

The one who says nothing is told everything (not that he
    cares). The one who dreamed me hasn't put me back.
    The sun and the moon, they rise on time. I still don't
    know how the engine works; I can splice a wire. That's
    about it.

The dream is my world, says the sick child. I am pure as these
    bed sheets. (He writes fatigue on the vast expanses.)
    I'm in your dream, says the wicked boy. The simple
    son has been decorated for objectivity. He who says
    nothing is still being told.

De Sade looks down through the bars of the Bastille. They
    have stepped up the slaughter of nobles.

The look of shock on an old friend's face

The look of shock on an old friend's face after years of not meeting, as if perhaps we were in a play, dressed for one of the final acts. The make-up of the years (infant, schoolboy, lover, soldier, judge of others, patriarch and ultimate old child) is on us. Those who remain the same and those who change their jaws. One has milky moons around the eyes or knotty knuckles. Many and varied are the studies in gray. The spectrum of whites amazes.

A generation moves in stateliness. It arrives like a pageant and passes down the street. The children sit on the curbs and watch. There are dignitaries and clowns, the men with medals and the cross-carriers. The owners walk abreast for the afternoon: they carry the banner which reads: the business of the world is—business. Manacled dictators walk alone through the crowded silence: four swordsmen guard them like points of the compass. The poets arrive on burros, bumping each other. Theologians packed in a hearse peer out like sickly popes. A phalanx of technologists singing the latest love songs in marching rhythms. Movie stars escorting diplomats (it's hard to tell them apart).

Nine of the greatest novelists, of ridiculous difference in height and girth. Two modern saints on litters. The generation proceeds to the cenotaph, the only common meeting place. In side streets the coming generation, not even looking, waits its turn and practices a new and secret language. (They think it's secret: that's what's so depressing.) Their hero is also gray and still in high school. He drives a hundred miles an hour into a tree.

Oriental, you give and give

Oriental, you give and give. No Christian ever gave like you. What is it you are giving morning and night, asking nothing in return? Pearls, silk cloths, books and scrolls, mother-of-pearl chopsticks, bronze cowbells, hand-painted poetry, tributes of every description. Flowers around my neck, morning, noon, and night: I am ready to vomit. You lay all Asia at my feet—where is your modern sense of values? You're not like a Frenchman, who gives as an investment. Not like an American whose gifts fall out of his pocket. Your gifts are permanent, an end in themselves. We'll cure you yet.

A rope of jasmine flowers round my neck at the airport, the embarrassing bow, the immaculate dark men come with their cargo. The frenzied Westerner grabs it all, the powder barrel stowed under the high altar, in case. The wise men continue to give: a sack of spices for the rotten meat of English queens; antimacassars; Zen.

It's as if you said, that's all I have to give, namely, the works. You never say, leave us alone. That's Western talk. You say, come for a swim in the old sky: my eyes are upside down. You say, the turtle can draw in its legs; the seer can draw in his senses; I call him illumined. In India eyes are never wide open. I throw a bucket of cold water over your continent. Get up from your bed of nails, you wise men of the East. I'm giving you a power plant for Christmas.

The rice around the lingam stone

The rice around the lingam stone will be distributed in the
dying sun to the unblessed poor. I bring neither rice
nor overpowering jasmine but only my full gaze of
love and loathing. With the beautiful Hindu woman I
drink in the phallus. On her face the trace of a sneer.
(She may be Christian.) Under the nine domes of the
Kali temple we make our way to the Divine Mother,
Savior of the Universe, Kali in basalt, in gold and
precious stones. She stands on Siva. A garland of
skulls hangs from her neck. In one of her four hands
a severed human head; with another she gives the sign
of peace. Her triple eyes bring peace or terror. This
was Ramakrishna's darling, standing on Siva, who lies
supine on the thousand-petaled silver-lotus.

He drank her smile till all was blue, that saint. He joined the
hands of all the gods. In his room a picture of Christ
as well. He reached the seventh plane at will.

Of love and death in the Garrison State I sing

Of love and death in the Garrison State I sing. From uni-
    formed populations rises the High Art, *Oedipus King*,
    the Nō, the ballerina bleeding in her slippers. At the
    Officer's Club adultery is rationed (their children are
    not allowed to play with guns; this helps whet their
    appetite). The ladies are discussing the chemical con-
    trol of behavior by radio waves: that will solve the
    problem of neighbors. Symposia on causes of desertion
    draw record-breaking crowds. The handsomer paci-
    fists are invited to the most sought-after cocktail
    parties. The women try their hand at them in the
    rumpus room; some progress reported. Waves of
    asceticism sweep the automobile industry. The mere
    sight of a Sam Browne belt, which used to inspire con-
    tempt, brings tears to the eyes of high-school boys. All
    flabby citizens are automatically put under surveil-
    lance. Chess problems supersede crap in the non-
    coms' barracks. The sacred number is Two: two
    parties, two powers sworn to mutual death, two poles
    of everything from ethics to magnetics. It's a balanced
    society.

Today the order goes out: all distant places are to be abol-
    ished: beachcombers are shot like looters. Established
    poets are forced to wear beards and bluejeans; they are
    treated kindly in bohemian zoos; mysterious stipends
    drift their way. They can trade soap for peyote at
    specified libraries. Children's prizes are given for es-
    says on the pleasures of crisis. Historians are awarded
    all the key posts in the foreign office. Sculptors who
    use old shrapnel are made the heads of schools of de-
    sign. Highways move underground like veins of ore.
    The Anti-Sky Association (volunteer contributions

only) meets naked at high noon and prays for color blindness.

"Color is a biological luxury."

Quintana lay in the shallow grave of coral

Quintana lay in the shallow grave of coral. The guns boomed stupidly fifty yards away. The plasma trickled into his arm. Naked and filthy, covered with mosquitoes, he looked at me as I read his white cloth tag. How do you feel, Quintana? He looks away from my gaze. I lie: we'll get you out of here sometime today.

I never saw him again, dead or alive. Skin and bones, with eyes as soft as soot, neck long as a thigh, a cross on his breastbone not far from the dog tags. El Greco was all I could think of. Quintana lying in his shallow fox-hole waiting to be evacuated. A dying man with a Spanish name equals El Greco. A truck driver from Dallas probably.

When the Japs were making the banzai charge, to add insult to death, they came at us screaming the supreme insult: *Babe Ruth, go to hell!* The Americans, on the other hand, when the Japs flew over dropping sticks of explosives, shouted into the air, as if they could hear: *Tojo, eat shit!*

Soldiers fall in love with the enemy all too easily. It's the allies they hate. Every war is its own excuse. That's why they're all surrounded with ideals. That's why they're all crusades.

The bourgeois poet

The bourgeois poet closes the door of his study and lights his
      pipe. Why am I in this box, he says to himself (al-
      though it is exactly as he planned). The bourgeois
      poet sits down at his inoffensive desk—a door with
      legs, a door turned table—and almost approves the
      careful disarray of books, papers, magazines and such
      artifacts as thumbtacks. The bourgeois poet is already
      out of matches and gets up. It is too early in the morn-
      ing for any definite emotion and the B.P. smokes. It is
      beautiful in the midlands: green fields and tawny
      fields, sorghum the color of red morocco bindings, dis-
      tant new neighborhoods, cleanly and treeless, and the
      Veterans Hospital fronted with a shimmering Indian
      Summer tree. The Beep feels seasonal, placid as a
      melon, neat as a child's football lying under the tree,
      waiting for whose hands to pick it up.

Office love

Office love, love of money and fight, love of calculated sex.
The offices reek with thin volcanic metal. Tears fall in
typewriters like drops of solder. Brimstone of bras-
sieres, low voices, the whirr of dead-serious play. From
the tropical tree and the Rothko in the Board Room to
the ungrammatical broom closet fragrant with waxes,
to the vast typing pool where coffee is being served by
dainty waitresses maneuvering their hand trucks,
music almost unnoticeable falls. The very telephones
are hard and kissable, the electric water cooler sweetly
sweats. Gold simmers to a boil in braceleted and sun-
burned cheeks. What ritual politeness nevertheless,
what subtlety of clothing. And if glances meet, if
shoulders graze, there's no harm done. Flowers, cele-
brations, pregnancy leave, how the little diamonds
sparkle under the psychologically soft-colored ceilings.
It's an elegant windowless world of soft pressures and
efficiency joys, of civilized mishaps—mere runs in the
stocking, papercuts.

Where the big boys sit the language is rougher. Phone calls
to China and a private shower. No paper visible anywhere. Policy is decided by word of mouth like gangsters. There the power lies and is sexless.

Lower the standard: that's my motto

Lower the standard: that's my motto. Somebody is always
putting the food out of reach. We're tired of falling off
ladders. Who says a child can't paint? A pro is somebody who does it for money. Lower the standards.
Let's all play poetry. Down with ideals, flags, convention buttons, morals, the scrambled eggs on the
admiral's hat. I'm talking sense. Lower the standards.
Sabotage the stylistic approach. Let weeds grow in the
subdivision. Putty up the incisions in the library façade, those names that frighten grade-school teachers,
those names whose U's are cut like V's. Burn the
Syntopicon and *The Harvard Classics*. Lower the
standard on classics, battleships, Russian ballet, national anthems (but they're low enough). Break
through to the bottom. Be natural as an American
abroad who knows no language, not even American.
Keelhaul the poets in the vestry chairs. Renovate the
Abbey of cold-storage dreamers. Get off the Culture
Wagon. Learn how to walk the way you want. Slump
your shoulders, stick your belly out, arms all over the
table. How many generations will this take? Don't
think about it, just make a start. (You have made a
start.) Don't break anything you can step around,
but don't pick it up. The law of gravity is the law of
art. You first, poetry second, the good, the beautiful
the true come last. As the lad said: We must love one
another or die.

Waiting in front of the columnar high school

Waiting in front of the columnar high school (the old ones look like banks, or rather insurance companies) I glance over the top of my book. The bells go off like slow burglar alarms; innumerable sixteeners saunter out. There's no running as in the lower schools, none of that helpless gaiety of the small. Here comes a surly defiance. As in a ritual, each lights a cigaret just at the boundary where the tabu ends. Each chews. The ones in cars rev up their motors and have bad complexions like gangsters. The sixteeners are all playing gangster.

The sea of subjectivity comes at you like a tidal wave, splashing the cuffs of middle-aged monuments. War is written on their unwritten faces. They try out wet dreams and wandering mind. They're rubbing Aladdin's lamp in the locker room. They pray for moments of objectivity as drunkards pray for the one that puts you out. They've captured the telephone centers, the microphones, the magazine syndicates (they've left the movies to us). I wait behind the wheel and spy; it's enemy territory all right. My daughter comes, grows taller as she approaches. It's a moment of panic.

But once at night in the sweet and sour fall I dropped her off at the football game. The bowl of light lit up the creamy Corinthian columns. A cheer went up from the field so shrill, so young, like a thousand birds in a single cage, like a massacre of child-brides in a clearing, I felt ashamed and grave. The horror of their years stoned me to death.

The dermatologist committed suicide

The dermatologist committed suicide, a good man, a sad man, with the hangdog mien of a proctologist.

Skin-watching, tricksy as palmistry, what medieval blips and scars, what outcroppings of thought! Maps of remorse, tattoos from voyages never undertaken, blueprints of literary cleverness, bad dreams of personal acid—the skin has wiles undreamed of by bacteria. Under the living continent of skin flows molten lava; heat spots and sinkings form, then violent eruption, appearance of crystals, the terrifying symmetry of disease. Thus the humiliation of itch- and scratch-lust, tearing of pleasure into pain, revenge of self and desecration of love.

So lay the mother of grown children, after the final consent to herself that the marriage was ended. The dermatologist pronounces the name of the rare sickness. She will lose her skin from top to toe, fingernails, toenails. Yet she will be like new, without a scar, made perfect after agony.

Italy spoiled California for me

Italy spoiled California for me. California spoiled Italy. Now I'm back in the Middle West, where I don't really belong. Nor can I go back East. Living in that Etruscan pine forest, maddened by too much sun, I watched the clouds gather up where Siena would be, and no rain came. Admittedly, it was the drying season. Heat of Florence on a Sunday afternoon. The horse almost fainted, pulling six in a buggy. Floods at Christmas in the Sacramento Valley: camellias floating in the gutters. The final fakery of palm trees in the palm-tree countries: emblem of grandiose injustice. In Nebraska the Russian olive, fruitless. Drunken smell of pine between Fredericksburg and Richmond and atop the Donner Pass. In Italy the scent barely perceptible, the bland Mediterranean, reddish yolks of eggs and dirty shells. The large soft Californians sideswiping the future: the small burning Italians endlessly plotting nothing. Everywhere the competition of boasting. Only the Navajo questioning time: what is a year? he asks. Does it have arms and legs? In Baltimore, walking in Victorian-movie snow it occurred to me: seek for the opposite. I'm for the Faustian supermarket. The opposite enthralls me. I refuse the wine of the locale. I smash customs like crockery. The Minnesota accent is music to my ears. The New Yorker is talking to me at top speed; the Frenchwoman flies into the conversation at breakneck; I slow them down with extreme modesty. Always at heart a central Californian, I nurse my own geography, miles of tomatoes, tons of sugar beets. I call a farm a ranch. But no palm trees.

The password of the twentieth century

The password of the twentieth century: Communications (as
    if we had to invent them). Animals and cannibals
    have communications; birds and bees and even a few
    human creatures, called artists (generally held to be
    insane). But the bulk of humanity had to invent
    Communications. The Romans had the best roads in
    the world, but had nothing to communicate over them
    except other Romans. Americans have conquered
    world-time and world-space and chat with the four
    corners of the earth at breakfast and have nothing to
    communicate except other Americans. The Russians
    communicate other Russians to the moon. The entire
    solar system is in the hands of cartoonists.

I am sitting in the kitchen in Nebraska and watching a
    shrouded woman amble down the market in Karachi.
    She is going to get her morning smallpox shot. It's cold
    and mental love they want: It's the mystic sexuality
    of Communications. Money was love. Power was love.
    Communications now are love. Sex-object of the tele-
    phone, let's kiss. The girl hugs the hi-fi speaker to her
    belly: it pours into her openings like gravy. In the
    spring, Hitler arises. This is the time of trampling.
    My japanned birds in the radioactive snow are calling.

A man appears at the corner of the street; I prepare myself for
    hospitality. Man or angel, welcome! But I am afraid
    and double-lock the door. On the occasion of the death
    of a political party, I send an epitaph by Western
    Union. I didn't go to the funeral of poetry. I stayed
    home and watched it on television. Moon in the bottom
    of the Steuben glass, sun nesting in New Mexican
    deserts—the primitive Christian communicated with a
    dirty big toe. He drew a fish in the dust.

It's lovely

It's lovely when one of them with a high jeweled hat and a crucifix the size of George Washington's hatchet gets caught in the act. We hug ourselves with happiness. We shrug when we hear that the alcoholic Jesuit is spending the winter in medical seclusion, that the rabbi is laying the Ladies Aid Society, the baldheaded Buddhist smuggling in machine guns. It's hard to hate them when they're so human. All the tales of Boccaccio wine us and dine us even on the deathbed, holier-than-thou. No matter how hard they try to rub it out, religion has love and kisses at the bottom. And because we know it has love at the bottom we follow the helmeted chaplain into battle. Onward, he yells, for God and country. Hurrah for Israel! Long live the Holy Roman Empire! Three cheers for Schleswig-Holstein and Carthage, Illinois! (That's where the Mormons got it in the neck.) In truth, there are two religions and two American flags, one for the rich and one for the poor. But they look so much alike we forget which one we are following. And after that there's church, the cosmos divided into calendar days and calendar hours. And in atheist nations the calendar of revolutions that failed. All of them fail, the heroes turned out of their graves. In the long run the only hope is for more human error on the part of the holy. Their sin is our salvation.

Abraham Lincoln wore the chimney hat

Abraham Lincoln wore the chimney hat and the smoke poured from the mills. Now we go nude in artificial summer. The sari is woman's most beautiful dress, though senseless in the snow. When men show their legs the skirts of women drop to the ankle. The longer the skirt the more of the bosom. A superior primitivism lays bare the nipples. But when in the entire history of man has he invented a more dreary uniform than the business suit? Here is the husk of the drone, unornamented, gray, the final comedown. Congo chief, back to your feathers!

Alas for the language of clothes, now written in code. We dress with scientific care, not to offend. Potentates were crushed by the weight of raiment. Though beauty makes its way through rags, extreme simplicity is a sign of power. Clothes are designed for the state of the hair. Those who afford elaborate hair are dressed in the ransom of princes. In prison and armies they first cut off your hair. The German haircut fits the iron heel. The king in curls wears tapestry. The barrister's wig bedecks the anachronism.

Children in uniform insult Jesus in heaven. A woman's undersilks smell fresh in the nostrils of God. Put flowers in thy hair. Keep hair in your armpits like the Italian women. Go naked in furs like Fraulein Else. You men, wear Texas hats: that's all that's left of the sale. And never mind the lilies of the field: the nuns dress well, whatever their religion. Puttees for men with doubtful calves. Nightgowns are nonsense. And don't forget the accessories.

The child who is silent

The child who is silent stands against his father, lovingly looking up at him as if to say without a trace of defiance: I
will speak when I have decided. He marches around
the table smiling intelligently, now and then deigning
to say something, perhaps "locomotive." It is somewhat frightening, a kind of rebuff to grownups. The
doctors smile and shrug. If the parents are worried
they don't display it. It's only like living in the last
house at the edge of the subdivision. There's a bit of
farm left and a highway beyond: if someone should
rattle the back door in the night . . . There is a child
of two minds who says nothing and who is drinking it
all in. Obviously happy, very much loved, handsome
and straight, laughing and playing, withholding that
gift we all abuse. In that room is a tower of books with
their backs to us, eloquently quiet too. Man is a torrent
of language, even in death. But visitors use longer
words. The little philosopher goes about his business.

This is the town where the railroads ended, the wagon trains
formed in the dry gray grass. It's this frontier of speech
we are always crossing. The locomotive is ridiculously
dying, lumbering off to the deep clay pits to settle
among the mastodon bones. The piano is thinking of
Mozart. On the very top, legs crossed, at ease, sits the
blue-eyed boy who holds his peace.

One of those idle autumn evenings

One of those idle autumn evenings on a street as harmless as
an Eskimo Pie, the young ones chatter on the porch
with their aunt, a woman of intelligence, as they say.
Someone across the street has died some days ago.
Once in a while a long wail of a female voice, as
though from a quite distant bedroom. It is somber and
full of dread, yet only a phrase, a Berlioz tune. We
discuss it thoroughly, how it trespasses on the music
of the street. And the aunt, taking the side of the
young perhaps, would quieten such grief, cure it more
quickly, have it get up and bathe and fill its lungs with
air and look at the world, though different now, but
still the only world.

Spoken too soon. Another week and her husband dies, a man
of reputation, in excellent health. Something has drawn
me to her porch again: the family is coming from the
cemetery. They carry her from the car; her screams rip
through the harmless street. Others are running from
other cars. By the end of the day half of her face is
turned in paralysis. For months her mouth lies in a
twist—that grief that parodies a smile.

Libraries

Libraries, where one takes on the smell of books, stale and attractive. Service with no motive, simple as U.S. Mail. Fountains and palms, armchairs for smokers. Incredible library where ideas run for safety, place of rebirth of forgotten anthems, modern cathedral for lovers. Library, hotel lobby for the unemployed, the failure, the boy afraid to go home, penniless. Switchboards for questioners: What do you know about unicorns? How do you address a duchess? Palladian architecture of gleaming glass and redwood. Window displays of this week's twelve best-sellers. Magnificent quarters of the director, who dines with names of unknown fame. Lavatories, rendezvous of desperate homosexuals. In the periodical room the newspapers bound with a stick, carried like banners of surrender to pale oak tables. Library, asylum, platform for uninhibited leaps. In the genealogy room the delicate perspiration of effete brains. Room also of the secret catalogue, room of unlisted books, those sought by police, manuscript room with the door of black steel, manuscripts stolen in delicate professional theft from abroad, sealed for seventy-five years. Sutras on spools of film. And all this courtesy and all this trust, tons of trash and tons of greatness, burning in time with the slow cool burning, burning in the fires of poems that gut libraries, only to rebuild them, more grand and Palladian, freer, more courteous, with cornerstones that say: Decide for yourself.

The two-year-old has had a motherless week

The two-year-old has had a motherless week. Mother has gone
to bring back the baby. A week is many many years.
One evening they bring the news to the playpen: a
child is born, you have a baby brother. The dark little
eyes consider this news and convey no message. One
day long after, they arrive in a taxi, father, mother,
bundle. The two-year-old observes from her blue
walker on the sunny sidewalk. She stares and turns
away on her wheels.

The father has gone to the other side of the world. He will
bring back strange presents to a strange house. The
little ones shyly wait their turn. Reconciliation is
gradual.

In Trenton, New Jersey, the soldiers sit in the innocuous bar.
It's three years since they saw the ones they wrote to.
They are all afraid to go home. One lives two blocks
away; he is very silent. Late in the afternoon, at an
ungiven signal, they get up and disperse, like criminals
perfectly trained for the job ahead.

In my brother's house when I left (whole histories ago) the
furniture was honeymoon fresh, gleam of ceramics;
soft beige carpets smelt like new-mown hay. With a
shock I see the carpet is worn; the sofa has settled;
books have changed places. A thousand days of words
have passed.

Time is mostly absences, oceans generally at peace, and lives
we love most often out of reach.

All tropic places smell of mold

All tropic places smell of mold. A letter from Karachi smells
of mold. A book I had in New Guinea twenty years ago
smells of mold. Cities in India smell of mold and dung.
After a while you begin to like it. The curry dishes in
the fine Bombay restaurant add the dung flavor. In the
villages dung patties plastered to the walls, the leaving of the cows the only cooking fuel. The smell rubs
into the blood.

Paris in the winter smells of wood smoke and fruit. Near the
Gare St. Lazare in the freezing dusk the crowds pour
slowly down the streets in every direction. A police van
the size of a Pullman car goes at a walking pace. The
gendarme keeps jumping down from the rear like a
streetcar conductor in the old days. He is examining
identity cards of pedestrians, especially the females. A
girl comes swinging along, her pocketbook in rhythm
with her behind. She is bareheaded and wears a rain-
coat. The gendarme examines her identity card. She is
motioned into the paddy wagon.

Salzburg, the castle smells of snow and peat. Baltimore, old
oaken bucket. Portsmouth, Virginia, roses and diesel
oil. Dublin, coal dust, saccharine whiskey, bitter
bodies. Damp gusts of Siena doorways. Warehouses
of Papeete, acrid smell of copra, fragipani, salt water
and mold. Smell of rotting water in Hollandia.

Unbreathable jungles, parks subtle and cool. Backstage the
ballet dancers wipe their sweat; "the entire stage stinks
like a stable." Sewer gas of beauty parlors. Electric
smell of hair in rut. Talcum powder, earliest recollec-
tion. Rome, the armpit of the universe.

From the top floor of the Tulsa hotel

From the top floor of the Tulsa hotel I gaze at the night beauty
of the cracking-plant. Candlelit city of small gas flames
by the thousands, what a lovely anachronism dancing
below like an adolescent's dream of the 1880's, the
holy gas redeemed from Baudelaire's mustachioed
curses. Elsewhere are the white lights of the age, but
here, like a millionaire who frowns on electricity, the
opulence of flame. Descending on Rome from the air at
night, a similar beauty: the weak Italian bulbs like
faulty rheostats yellowly outline the baroque curves
of the Tiber, the semicircles of the monstrous Vatican,
endless broken parabolas.

The cracking-plant is equally palatial. Those oil men in the
silent elevator, like princes with their voices of natural
volume, their soft hats and their name-drops (like
balloons of words in the mouths of caricatures in political cartoons), men of many mansions. The doors
of the room are mahogany. Through one which adjoins
and is locked I hear the guttural laughter of undress,
neither leisurely nor quick, indistinct wording, and all
is silent but a woman's moan. Now it rises like the grip
of pain; it is almost loud; it is certainly sincere, like the
pent-up grief of deep relief; now it is round, now
vibrant, now it is scaly as it grows. (Then it steps off
into nothingness.)

I stand awed in my stocking-feet and move respectfully toward
the window, as a man in an art gallery moves toward a
more distant masterpiece to avoid the musical chatter
of intruders. The cracking-plant sails on through the
delicate Oklahoma night, flying the thousand hot flags
of Laputa.

There's a Parthenon in Nashville

There's a Parthenon in Nashville large as life, the only perfect
    replica. Greeks resent it probably: it sits flat on the
    ground, like a plane crash reconstructed. It's not that
    famous derelict in space (blasted to bits by a Venetian
    general). It's not real marble but the brownish con-
    crete has the rusty tinge of the Pentelikon. The
    brownish yellow came from the Potomac. The British
    Government cast these Elgin marbles.

Stepping from your car beneath the West Pediment, you fall
    back foot after foot. It crouches over you, a dark red
    turmoil, savage, barbaric—how can this be! Those
    columns like piano legs, prototype of Middle Western
    banks, and brazen doors the biggest in the world. Only
    in the Naos where the goddess is gone (she's never
    been found, like Eve) the pallid beauty dawns and
    spreads like cunningly concealed electric light. The
    beautiful goddess of ivory and gold, torn into shreds
    for dagger grips or crucifixes, has no single worshiper
    left on the face of the earth, it says at the close of the
    guidebook. It was her temple, then it was a church,
    then it was a mosque (even with minaret!). Now it's
    the temple of art. We buy it and sell it fifty times a day.
    It's the warehouse of the spirit, a faulty translation.

You, Morosini, dread doge of Venice, what was it like when
    you saw the Explosion? A direct hit if there ever was
    one! And the Turks thought Athena would protect
    their gunpowder.

Hart Crane

Hart Crane, though handicapped, did well with the burlesk:
all but her belly buried in the floor. Magdalene? Perhaps. In Kansas City I pay my respects to the dying
art. The theater is in ruins, the ticket-taker only half-
conscious. Wine took him long ago. The carpet in the
aisle is ripped; twice I snag my foot. The rank air
smells of disinfectant. All seats are vacant except the
first two rows. These are lit up as in a Rembrandt picture, the glowing center of the operation. I sit down
inches from the drum. It lifts my hair each second it
is smashed. The snare drum hisses and the block
clicks. The cymbal crazes.

She's halfway through, already down to the sash that hangs
like a silk muffler between her buttocks. She gyrates
with an expert beat, more round than sharp. Small-
breasted, her nipples glitter with stardust—some local
ordinance. She is very pretty, not what you would expect, almost indifferently dancing her career. Cold
flows from her steady limbs; stately she spreads her
thighs for the climactic grind, when at the highest
throw she slips her final string, holding one hand over
the part like a live fig leaf, and flittering her fingers off
—and we are there, and she is all but hairless.

Our faces light up with intelligence.

Why poetry small and cramped

Why poetry small and cramped, why poetry starved and mean, thin-lipped and sunken-cheeked? Why these pams, these narrow-shouldered negatives? (The best we can say is that they're seed catalogs.) And why those staring eyes, so carefully fixed on the photographic plate? Why no lips at all but in their stead the practiced line of anger and the clamped jaw? Why always the darkening halo, so seemingly satanic? (The best we can say is that they are trying to mirror our lives. Do they know our lives? Can they read past the symbols of our trade?) Why so much attention to the printed page, why the cosmetology of font and rule, meters laid on like fingernail enamel? Why these lisping indentations, Spanish question marks upside down? Why the attractive packaging of stanza? Those cartons so pretty, shall I open them up? Why the un-American-activity of the sonnet? Why must grown people listen to rhyme? How much longer the polite applause, the tickle in the throat?

What will fatten you, skinny little book? What will put lead in your pencil? All of you dust-collecting seed catalogs, to the Goodwill you go, to the broad stench of the paper mill! Seed catalog, go pulp yourself!

Poems, flowers of language, if that's what you are, grow up in the air where books come true. And you, thin packet, let your seed fly, if you have any.

Broken bottles hard-set in cement

Broken bottles hard-set in cement, green glass, brown glass,
wavy white and blue, they glitter down the street like
distant peaks. I call it St. Mary's of the broken bottle
necks. It's the black belt of the town and the old con-
vent. The mossy wall surmounted with jags and hates
of glass, hard-set in cement, ledges of rotten ice, yet
feminine.

When the sun strikes these fragments like stained glass, what
do the sisters feel who walk within these walls? Here
are no pictured saints leaded together from the days of
blood. Here are the ugly claws of chastity, the long
fingernails of theological grief, the severed tendons,
castrations for all these perpetually mourning virgins,
those lovely Héloïses awakened by knives, deliciously
composing love letters forever.

Who drank from these bottles, cracked them so carefully and
fixed them in the brick?

In a fine Connecticut living room I saw a Calder once of broken
bottles strung in an empty frame. The necks hung free,
turning slightly on their slender wires.

The living rooms of my neighbors

The living rooms of my neighbors are like beauty parlors, like
night-club powder rooms, like international airport
first-class lounges. The bathrooms of my neighbors are
like love nests—Dufy prints, black Kleenex, furry
towels, toilets so highly bred they fill and fall without
a sigh (why is there no bidet in so-clean America?).
The kitchens of my neighbors are like cars: what
gleaming dials, what toothy enamels, engines that
click and purr, idling the hours away. The basements
of my neighbors are like kitchens; you could eat off the
floor. Look at the furnace, spotless as a breakfront,
standing alone, prize piece, the god of the household.

But I'm no different. I arrange my books with a view to their
appearance. Some highbrow titles are prominently displayed. The desk in my study is carefully littered;
after some thought I hang a diploma on the wall, only
to take it down again. I sit at the window where I can
be seen. What do my neighbors think of me—I hope
they think of me. I fix the light to hit the books. I lean
some rows one way, some rows another.

A man's house is his stage. Others walk on to play their bit
parts. Now and again a soliloquy, a birth, an adultery.

The bars of my neighbors are various, ranging from none at
all to the nearly professional, leather stools, automatic
coolers, a naked painting, a spittoon for show.
The businessman, the air-force captain, the professor with
tenure—it's a neighborhood with a sky.

After the war

After a war the boys play soldier with real weapons. This is a
real hand grenade, a pineapple. The killing stuff has
been removed but the pin remains to pull out and push
in. There is a clip to hang it from your belt. The pineapple is a red-brown iron the color of—a pineapple,
very heavy to hold, very heavy to throw, though small.
All the boys own a pineapple. The squares are cut deep
in the metal fruit. When it explodes, we say, you have
diced pineapple and dying men and a hole in the
ground.

The dummy rifles are dark-brown wood. Every part is round
and smooth. There is no metal, no trigger assembly.
The dummy muzzle comes to a rubber end like a
truncheon or a heavy walking stick. It is five feet tall
and too heavy for boys to hold out straight in the
standing position, but fine to hold prone or stand in
the corner of the bedroom.

The shallow helmet is rough to the feel, a greenish basin with
a cocky steel brim. Inside, the webbing is leather to fit
the skull and carry the shock. Mine has a handsome
dent in the top, a round dent with a crease at the bottom. There is a delicate line of rust in the crease, a
close call for somebody.

Today we play on the gray wooden battleship built on the grass
for the sailors' drills. This must be the biggest toy in
the world, a full-sized ship, a ship out of water, all
above ground, without a keel. The Naval Base is always open to boys. The Naval Base is filled with
flowered walks and neat straight lines and white-
washed curbs. The officers' houses are white and face

the Bay. The wooden battleship is a school. It never rocks but runs up fluttering flags. The ship browses at peace among the flowers of the Naval Base. The Shore Police in their sentry boxes at the main entrance don't even notice us as we come and go. We are part of the game.

The shell-shocked newsman stomps down Granby Street, shouting commands and thumping his truncheon-stick on the ground. Nobody laughs at him; everyone says he is harmless. The fits of stomping and shouting commands come once or twice a day. Then he subsides in a truce with himself. When there are parades he stands at attention.

Leaving the troopship, men hacked at walls, slit mattresses, broke pipes, gouged at lounge-room ornamentation, middle-class British taste for luxury liners, made minor desecrations of the great gray leviathan. On this voyage of forty days and forty nights the Americans consumed a quarter of a million Coca-Colas, the sergeant says, and spits between his feet.

The General returns with the power of a god. His disgrace is a triumph. The world pours at his feet like a tide; it swirls through cities and engulfs skyscrapers. Men become frightened at their own frenzy. In Chicago the cheering and weeping are endemic, maniacal. The General is handsome, arrogant, and wrong. Such a General might be the President. He leaves his car to lay a wreath on a bridge across the poisonous Chicago River. He delivers his profile to rich and poor. In the war his communiqués always mentioned God. We hated him.

The History of Philosophy professor

The History of Philosophy professor is a fashion plate of su-
periority. There's not a note in sight: the desk in front
of him is a useless prop left over by some amateur
company. His timing is as elegant as that of the Buda-
pest String Quartet. Small, handsome, dressed with
the quiet of a minor prince who made off with the
money, he never lights a cigaret until the question
period. And never superior to the questioner—you
would have to be his wife to know when he is impatient. In war he wears a Navy uniform of very seri-
our rank.

Now we have shot Zeno's arrow, with inexplicable excitement.
We have made a choice between Parmenides and
Heraclitus. Myself, I write a paper on Lord Herbert
and Thomas Jefferson. Spring comes with Schopen-
hauer. Exams flush everything out of our minds.

It begins when you say: I am not that and that is not me. I'm
only another that in the world. But I would like to
know about that that. I find a use for that. It begins
when you say: those are the terrors of women and
children. Those are the poems of the sick. Philosophy
always defeating itself with its own rules, chasing after
chemistry with Wait, Wait! And holy men digging
elephant traps. When you know this history, what
do you know? You know the history of trying to know.

What then is Other—other-brother-mother . . .

When suffering is everywhere, that is of the nature of belief

When suffering is everywhere, that is of the nature of belief. When the leaders are corrupted, Pope or Commissar, nor do the people flicker an eyelash, that is of the nature of belief. When there are anniversaries of battle or martyrdom, that is of the nature of belief. When there is the slogan Credo quia absurdum or intellectual proof of the existence of God, that is of the nature of belief. When priests pray for victory and generals invoke heaven, when prisons fill with children, that is of the nature of belief. When the word *evil* appears in newspapers, *moral* in the mouths of policemen, *culture* in the prepared speeches of politicians, all that is of the nature of belief. Belief makes blood flow. Belief infects the dead with more belief. Now it flows in our veins. Now it floats in the clouds.

I am an atheist who says his prayers

I am an atheist who says his prayers.

I am an anarchist, and a full professor at that. I take the loyalty oath.

I am a deviate. I fondle and contribute, backscuttle and brown, father of three.

I stand high in the community. My name is in *Who's Who.* People argue about my modesty.

I drink my share and yours and never have enough. I free-load officially and unofficially.

A physical coward, I take on all intellectuals, established poets, popes, rabbis, chiefs of staff.

I am a mystic. I will take an oath that I have seen the Virgin. Under the dry pandanus, to the scratching of kangaroo rats, I achieve psychic onanism. My tree of nerves electrocutes itself.

I uphold the image of America and force my luck. I write my own ticket to oblivion.

I am of the race wrecked by success. The audience brings me news of my death. I write out of boredom, despise solemnity. The wrong reason is good enough for me.

I am of the race of the prematurely desperate. In poverty of comfort I lay gunpowder plots. I lapse my insurance.

I am the Babbitt metal of the future. I never read more than half of a book. But that half I read forever.

I love the palimpsest, statues without heads, fertility dolls of the continent of Mu. I dream prehistory, the invention of dye. The palms of the dancers' hands are vermillion. Their heads oscillate like the cobra. High-caste woman smelling of earth and silk, you can dry my feet with your hair.

I take my place beside the Philistine and unfold my napkin. This afternoon I defend the Marines. I goggle at long cars.

Without compassion I attack the insane. Give them the horse-whip!

The homosexual lectures me brilliantly in the beer booth. I can feel my muscles soften. He smiles at my terror.

Pitchpots flicker in the lemon groves. I gaze down on the plains of Hollywood. My fine tan and my arrogance, my gray hair and my sneakers, O Israel!

Wherever I am I become. The power of entry is with me. In the doctor's office a patient, calm and humiliated. In the foreign movies a native, shabby enough. In the art gallery a person of authority (there's a secret way of approaching a picture. Others move off). The high official insults me to my face. I say nothing and accept the job. He offers me whiskey.

How beautifully I fake! I convince myself with men's room jokes and epigrams. I paint myself into a corner and escape on pulleys of the unknown. Whatever I think at the moment is true. Turn me around in my tracks; I will take your side.

For the rest, I improvise and am not spiteful and water the plants on the cocktail table.

When I dismissed you, friend, why did I do that? The Judas
 in me is strong. With an effort I regain my loyalty,
 and lose it again. These virtues incapacitate me. The
 solitude of the masochist is mine.

Albatross of a prize, you who married me to a newspaper, you
 who made me a government, why can't I thank you?

Kindness of deep hostility, my patience of a saint, endless
 capacity for love—mother, did I have the breast really?
 (But you gave me girls in your own likeness.)

This laissez-aller, this Traumdeutung—am I really a poet? Do
 I give a damn? That too I betray. I cross my fingers
 and exclude bedfellow death. I rub the icebox with my
 swimming thighs. I embrace the white rhinoceros; I
 propose to toilets.

What right have I to be healthy? What right have I to escape?
 And what is it I have escaped? I explore opportunities.
 (The rising sun sits on my other head. My cancer is
 blooming.)

I insist on the middle-aged poet. Brats of the drunken boat,
 centurions in the pay of Congress, gray and forgetful,
 purposefully stupid—God bless you, and Congress.

Marvelously recapitulating man, the child, reviving literature,
 invents religion. The dog flops on the floor with graceful disgust.

Goldfish, I loved you. When you died I cried. I'm no biologist.
 I did my best. I know. I overfed you. I was warned on
 the box. (The air-force officer has a tropical tank. His
 fishes glitter like a jewelry store.)

*   *   *

New York, my love, we never went to bed. (You never asked
     me.) New York, my Jewess, you read me Kierkegaard
     on the subway, standing up. I didn't give you a chance
     to kill me, N.Y.

Chicago, what did I do to you? What's another stab in the
     back, Chicago?

New York, killer of poets, do you remember the day you passed
     me through your lower intestine? The troop train
     paused under Grand Central. That line of women in
     mink coats handed us doughnuts through the smutty
     windows. They were all crying. For that I forgive
     New York. (We smuggled a postcard off at New
     Haven.)

Chicago, smothered in boredom and pigs: your Gothic uni-
     versities, your Portuguese wines, your bad baseball.

New York, island of prisons. New York of a billion black
     Rimbauds. Chicago of dreamy cardinals.

What was it like, New York, when the skyscrapers were
     white? New York of Hart Crane. Harlem of Lorca.

Chicago of T.S. Eliot (his city). Chicago of bad impulses.

*   *   *

All things remain to be simplified. I find I must break free of
     the poetry trap.

The books I hunger for are always out, never to be returned:
     illuminations, personal bibles, diatribes, chapters de-
     nied acceptance in scripture, Tobit blinded by sparrows
     muting warm dung in his eyes, immense declarations
     of revolt, manuals of the practice of love.

I seek the entrance of the rabbit hole. Maybe it's the door that has no name.

My century, take savagery to your heart. Take wooden idols, walk them through the streets. Bow down to Science.

My century that boils history to a pulp for newspaper, my century of the million-dollar portrait, century of the decipherment of Linear B and the old scrolls, century of the dream of penultimate man (he wanders among the abandoned skyscrapers of Kansas; he has already forgotten language), century of the turning-point of time, the human wolf pack and the killing light.

*   *   *

Crazy-clean, our armies and bodies. Crazy-clean the institutions of the mind. Crazy-clean Washington, D.C.

The generals say: mop up, no sweat, cordon sanitaire, liquidate, flush, wipe out.
How many have escaped the prison of Art? Who has not been extradited? Through the blue grid of technique we read the wild faces.

Stanza means room, with bars on it. Form means shape, beaten and maimed. It is done, ingeniously done, immortally done. For a century or two it pleases and instructs.

Now and again, one of the slaves escapes. His eyes are put out with platinum hatpins.

To escape to America. How is it there? Do the bluecoats smile?

The little ones file into the classroom. The giggling dies down. They salute the flag. They bow their heads. Childhood is over. When the air raid sounds they crouch on the floor like Moslems. It's only for practice of course.

I tell the secret of the starving artist. A day after he died the chauffeurs knocked at the door.

Poets of early death, who overturned the boat? Physician John Keats, cure thyself!

Lists of the mad and bibles of the damned. Dictionaries of suicide, card indexes of the compulsive revolutionaries, Protestant cemeteries of sacred remains. Beatification of the Dutchman's ear. Under the dome of poetry an array of saints as broken as christological glass. Martyrology of prosodists. Mariolatry of Hebrews. Every twilight of the mind for sale.

Counterfeiters, defenders of hell-gate. The intentionally mad, aristocrats of the verb, apologists of exile, culture nationalists, founders of the Next Phase.

Studies of the decrease of light. Paintings of right angles. Poems with square edges. Literary quarterlies refined from steel.

* * *

The teacher recites her lesson: the poem lifts me; it tips my arrows. No matter the horror; it washes us, the blood-washed poem.

The teacher recites her lesson: this is reality; this is the ideal. This is the touch of God. My Muse, my mother, my fertile one. (A slow leak in the footnotes: the goddess bleeds apace.)

Why do you paint your lips? Is it time to eat?

The tigress rolls its cubs. The dainty sparrow, proletarian bird, lights on the horse turd, a golden bun. The mouse in the trap has exquisite fur. I touch it with my fingers before I lift it from the drawer on its well-made mouse-trap. The vertebra of the rattlesnake lies in the palm of my hand, a masterpiece of subtle bone. Where did you get it? The doll pouts: the child is learning a picture. You have to be taught to *read* a picture. The savage looks at the photograph of himself; he turns it sideways and upside-down. Why doesn't it register?

The class convenes in the library attic. I introduce myself and throw their books out of the window. We will write a poem together, I say. (I see the gothic in their eyes.) It turns out nicely.

My Utamaro is pea green. I see what Vincent saw.

Sunday cut into colored squares, *Chicago Tribune*, Japanese print of future generations, I collect your yellows and washy blues. Bold line of Dick Tracy, Lautrec of murder, sexless, decisive, one riddle solved, a fresh body produced. Your palindromes, a villain named Etah. Evil, said Carroll, is live spelled backwards.

Permanent orphan of generations, has daddy gone to fight the Communists with his private army and his diamond stickpin? Carrot-top orphan who still says *Hark!*

Cornbeef and cabbage man, pining for the brownstone days. Matronly Maggie with a rolling pin. (Pogo and Peanuts leave me cold.)

Sirens with black lips and identical faces. Fly-boys in the Orient; regulation uniforms.

Tillie and Mack in the Kinsey Collection. In New Guinea the Japanese propaganda drawings dropped from a Zero: Yank, this is what civilian is doing to your wife back home. (Showing what.) Colors of Utamaro.

Frank Merriwell at Yale. Tom the fun-loving Rover. Tom
    Swift and his electric grandmother (joke). Alger,
    Henty, S. S. Van Dine.

"Patterns" by Amy Lowell. And in Virginia, *Southern Prose
    and Poetry*.

Books for the sake of shelves. Encyclopedia of railroad engi-
    neering, sixty-seven volumes, fold-out plates of boilers,
    piston assembly. The Waverly novels, dark tomes
    maroon and brown to handle on a rainy day. Balzac
    complete, unread. *The Harvard Classics*, mean, un-
    provocative, *Veritas* stamped on the backbone.

                    *   *   *

Poem, is it de rigueur to descend to hell? Will you lose your
    pedigree?

How businesslike is convention. What slag the prodigies of
    the epic mind. How little human the heroes and angels.

Tell me again what tragedy is. I can never remember.

Because the king is a fool and the lady a bitch; because a
    woman butchers her children to spite her husband; or
    a man makes love to his mother by mistake—shall I
    descend to hell?

Because the dollar tips the scales; or certain languages are
    dead; the nobility bankrupt; because the government
    has awarded you teeth—shall I descend to hell?

I descend and find the usual evidence. And Paul made love
    to Frances and they burn forever.

Where are you taking me, Alighieri? I have a different religion. I go with Geoffrey to the house of April. Gottfried of Strassburg, give us the gutsy Tristan.

Children play on the gorgeous baldaquin, climbing the marble vines while the mothers kneel, eating the Body. The priest moves rapidly from mouth to mouth. Black and white, the barbaric tower rears over history. It's no playground.

The bloodshot Germans enter the Forum in shorts. Proudly they gaze on the fine destruction.

In Bombay the vegetarians storm the hotel: "You are eating the flesh of the god!" A dirty cow stands in the doorway of the office building. A Hindu gives it a kick in the rump and sends it off in the rain.

I teach the emotions. The head is a hugeness already. Sin is ruled out. A tropic laugh splits heaven up the middle.

The disciplinarians stalk between the flowers. The whips crash on the bitten fingernails. It's war from the start. The books are weighted with lead. The catechism demands more algebra. Down on your knees.

Who teaches manners of fear? Who teaches reverence of wealth? Why so many books? What fabulous detail, what attractive bindings! Did you take the Intelligence Test this morning? Would you like to learn Russian?

The mind, the mind, cleaned like a car, purring like a fan. And the feelings matted and stuck, scratching the lice of love.

Do you hate your face? It is your sex you hate. Worship has pigged your eyes.

*   *   *

O love, phenomenon of attention, hear me out! I hold the
    shaving mirror to all:

To you at breakfast with folded newspaper,

You with the telephone in your hand and the glass name on the
    door,

You the alumnus, recipient of telegraphed congratulation,

You on election night, you in the driver's seat,

You in dutiful coitus, you in social drunkenness, you in
    parental storm;

At the cornerstone, near the triumphal arch, on the cruise
    deck, in the ad for bitters,

In the photograph of the first lieutenant, signed "Ages ago,"

In the vestry room with the males and the white flower,

In the waiting room of the daffodil maternity ward,

At the elegant tent beside the open grave (the coffin glows like
    a fine piano);

To you saluting, you baring your head, you holding the scissor
    to the early rose—

Did you know the damasked walls gave way so rottenly, the
    gilted wood so mealy with fatigue?

Did you see the estates divided and plowed and the monstrous
    houses opened to view for your sad Sundays?

Aren't you the popular song of God in the formstone churches, you of ideals and virtues, responsible, lovable, disciplined, free?

Isn't it you you mutter against, with your fuzzed haircut in your wife's bosom?

Citizen, is your glorious revolution over and done with?

And you, my country, how does it feel to be They?

What are those objects on which our eyes are frozen?

Flag on the candy-factory grammar school;

Eternal light hung from a silver chain above the Ark in the synagogue;

Samurai sword in the French admiral's possession (to be given to a poet on a state occasion);

Rectilinear façade of Greek; font of the Hebrew; spittle of the christer contorting on the bare ground;

Finder of inscapes; critique of frameless abstractions; voyeurs of myth;

Hypnotized lovers; Napoleonic captains of copper mines; editors of quack compendia of knowledge;

All worshipers, all fanatics, all absorbed in the object which is really you,

You who descry the streamings of life as other and beyond;

You strapped to your muscles (is the culture-gag in your teeth?);

Altars, uniforms of every description, detritus of battles, delirium of ethics, codes of the good, new wars, new medals, new masterpieces forged for the market;

Heavy stone of your overturned lives, what crawling dreams!

What is it you are trying to become, men of my species?

Homo normalis, blind as a bat, that music you hear is coming from you. Where did you study the physics of the epic? What is this eternal conspiracy of distraction? Why are the sick the most articulate? Poetry weaving at the bar, go home. Somebody call a cab.

Who are these that compound the mystery? Tell me about the Dewey Decimal System.

Do something about the sour smell of schools. Call the Americans!

Herewith I abolish up and down. Future and past for those with radial vision.

Everything everywhere has been decided in everyone's favor.

I end on the dead level and peter out. Is it time for the curtain? Shall we applaud at the end of the second movement?

*   *   *

I love Nowhere where the factories die of malnutrition.

I love Nowhere where there are no roads, no rivers, no interesting Indians,

Where history is invented in the History Department and there are no centennials of anything,

Where every tree is planted by hand and has a private tutor,

Where the "parts" have to be ordered and the sky settles all
questions,

Where travelers from California bitch at the backwardness and
New Yorkers step on the gas in a panic,

Where the grass in winter is gray not brown,

Where the population diminishes.

Here on the boundary of the hired West, equidistant from
every tourist office, and the air is washed by distance,
here at last there is nothing to recommend.

May no one ever attempt a recommendation; Chicago be as far
as Karachi.

Though the warriors come with rockets, may they fall off the
trucks.

May the voting be light and the clouds like a cruise and the
criminal boredom enter the district of hogs.

I love Nowhere where the human brag is a brag of neither
time nor place,

But an elephant house of Smithsonian bones and the white
cathedrals of grain,

The feeding-lots in the snow with the steers huddled in sym-
metrical misery, backs to the sleet,

To beef us up in the Beef State plains, something to look at.

*   *   *

To the poor (aux pauvres) crime alone (le crime seul) opens
    (ouvre) les portes de la vie (the doors of life). Entire
    libraries of music are hurled in the gutters: the G.I.'s
    are looking for bottles. The Bavarian Venus is snatched
    baldheaded.

I have a big sister; she has mighty breasts. She writes poems
    for the immigration office. Her crotch is on the four-
    teenth floor. La géante, la géante!

Standing at the pure white rail, stately we pass you, and the
    classes mingle as if by degree. At the last buoy the
    discreet signs begin to take effect: First Class, Second
    Class. My brazen sister swirling her nightgown, green
    as the spouts of Chartres. Her comb is combing my
    lice (but I have no lice). Her apron is hitched up in
    front. She stands on a full-sized bank.

Across the iambic pentameter of the Atlantic (the pilot
    dropped, the station wagon in the hold) we sail to the
    kingdom of Small. Is it cheaper there? Can I buy a
    slave?

This is the camera with the built-in lie. This is the lens that
    defies the truth. There's nothing for it but to write the
    large bad poem in middle-class magic. Poem con-
    demned to wear black, be quoted in churches, versatile
    as Greek. Condemned to remain unsung by criminals.

This Slavic typist

This Slavic typist had high cheekbones and gigantic mouth
and a voice like sleep. That Kyoto hostess naturally.
Marlene, Medea, and my wife, women proud as Tar-
tars, women with marvelous voices and big feet have
high cheekbones and dress their hair to a height. In
overcivilized rooms you will always find one or two.

The Victorian houri had an oval face, a drooping silkiness of
flesh like ottomans. She melted away in the dawn of
the century. A drunken poet roars out across the room:
are you a tit man or an ass man? I mumble in reply:
high cheekbones.

Verlaine compares the buttocks and the breasts: buttocks the
holy throne of the indecencies. Breasts savored by
drunken lips and the tongue. Buttocks with their
ravine of rose and somber shadow, where desire prowls
when it goes crazy. Breasts proud and victorious,
breasts heavy and powerful. Buttocks, beloved cush-
ions, with a voluptuous fold for your face or your sex.
O holy quaternity of sacred breasts and august buttocks.

Poets with high cheekbones, Rimbaud, Pasternak.

In the second-best hotel in Tokyo

In the second-best hotel in Tokyo the chambermaids are chasing the chamberboys. Laughter tinkles up and down the halls. The elevator girls sing it when they say: ten floor, please; seven floor, please (their faces like gardenias). The cashier's fingers race back and forth over the counting frame.

In the first-best Western-style hotel in Kyoto I describe to the barmaid how to make a Bloody Mary, and am proud. I walk through the fish market with the editor of *The Kenyon Review*. The fishes are displayed like masterpieces. This is more beautiful than the Louvre.

I fall in love with the torii gate, graceful salmon arms, the light rust color. From now on it's my Parthenon. The wooden golden palace floats on its pond. The nightingale floors warn me of my assassins. I sleep like an Oriental.

Zen is on the verge of being discovered. We climb to the famous abstract garden and study the sand designs and the rocks. To my companion I say: how do they fix it without messing it up? He laughs at my westernization.

As for the haiku, you can make it tough. It isn't exactly a valentine, except in the States.

The poet takes the voyage

The poet takes the voyage to the New Cytherea. Fifty miles
from little Papeete he and his girl have rented a
thatched hut. He says the name of the district over
and over: Taravao, Taravao. The hut is right on the
beach; water laps at the pilings. The whole front opens
crazily out and is propped up by a stake. The roof is
pandanus, very brown and dusty, a house of straw. No
sooner have they entered when the poet grabs up a
witch's broom and begins to sweep. The girl hangs
batiks on the wall. There are spiders big as your hand.
Frozen with terror the poet smashes them.

Over the water rises Moorea, blue-mauve with lots of red, as
the painter saw it. The poet sweeps and arranges like
a woman. He lays out books. The hut is ready at last;
they lean out of the open wall and worship the world.
They make love on the crunchy bed. Later the natives
bring bananas as a gift. Their movements are slow and
peaceful, their French is soft and broad. Inside the
coral reef the swimming is perfect. They shop in
Papeete. They bank at the Bank of Indo-China. Everything is exotic, even the nuns. At the Post Office a
crowd of French sailors are arguing grimly. Spain is at
war with itself. It has started today. It is even here.

There is only one movie: *Tabu* by Murnau. The natives return to it like a church. We go there. It is great like
literature.

Wood for the fireplace

Wood for the fireplace, wood for the floor, what is the life
span? Sometimes before I lay the log on the fire I
think: it's sculpture wood, it's walnut. Maybe someone would find a figure in it, as children find faces in
the open fire (I never have). Then I lay it on the
flames like a heretic, where it pauses a moment, then
joins in the singing. There's oak in this cord too. My
floor is oak. I watched them lay this floor, for a vastly
slower fire. The grooved pieces are fitted together; it's
more like a game than work; there are many choices.
The grain falls arbitrarily, dark streaks and light,
dots and dashes, swirls and striped shields.

Dead wood can last forever (is it dead)? Dead wood glows
in palaces, rosy and dark as masterpieces. I worship
wood, split my own logs in the driveway, using a
maul and iron wedges. The cracking-apart is hard and
sweet. I touch wood for my superstition, using five
fingers as an extra precaution. My gods would all be
wood if I had gods, not stone or gold or Peter's smooth-
kissed toe.

In woodless Italy houses are built without a sound, no ring
of hammer on nail or wood. All is quiet, stone laid
upon stone, rubble, cement, tufa, travertine, tile.
Rarely you see some show-off house of wood, exotic
among the blinding stucco, soft among the cool and
stony facings, the marbly infinitude.

In a single motion

In a single motion, a snap of the hand, you take the white
bishop with your black knight, taking-replacing. It's
neat, like trigger work, the click of the chessmen
speaking in passing, like the hammers of empty re-
volvers. Well, uncle who taught me the courtly game,
who sat with experts over silent boards, I never made
the grade. I play as badly now that I'm gray as I did
those years before I shaved. My chess plateau was
never a high one. No matter. Still, I can beat my
children when we play, which is practically never.
When we do, and I capture a pawn or a rook with a
click, taking-replacing, I think of your house, the
pipes, the dice, the trinkets, curios ("novelties" they
were called). Your business, pipes and novelties, not
very lucrative but treasure-trove of kids. Your sad
blond face, so kind, politically angry, yet easy to
laugh—you were not at home in this country, scholar
manqué, drifting apart from the richer and richer
relations. Your foreign accent perhaps, your synagogue training leading to nowhere. There was that
about you of the disengaged, the saint (using the word
advisedly and well), the Jewish radiance of a Chagall.
The rich ones never played chess, the poetry of war,
nor grunted sadly at the news. In America, scholars
are thrown into the street or made to stand behind
cool counters, thumping, unthumping the mighty bolts
of cloth. Good cloth at that but not for the torah.

Not at all my favorite author

Not at all my favorite author, Kipling described Chicago once:
the water is the water of the Hooghly, and the air is
dirt. And as famous a poet of New England whom I
drive to the station: it's a grand city. (*Grand*, a nine-
teenth-century word.)

Under its permanent umbrella of travail, Chicago swirls in
grit. Smuts drift in the sky, penetrate window glass,
light on petals of window-box flowers, turning gera-
niums pansy-black. All is charred, all is furred with
dirt, the sky winter and summer streaked like the sky-
light of the grandest railroad station, basilicas of practical kings.

But now we take leave forever by car, driving in early morning
south, miraculously out from under the soiled umbrella, south and more south in the dead blue winter
light, south and west in the snow-light, till the snow
rots in Arkansas, then west again, the holy direction.

Far from the Chicago cave, spring comes facing toward summer, such summer as happens only in one place in a
given country.

There is a rise (where is it on the map?), on one side America
and on the other, California. There you look down on
promised advertisements of green come true, green for
the eating, money-green, and the rows of the royal
palm for welcome, official, frightening. The Californians live in California. The money groves are green.
American is a suburb of California et cetera et cetera.

America is Hooghly.

Little tendon, tiny as a hair

Little tendon, tiny as a hair—tinier, the surgeon said—they couldn't catch you on the operating table. Three hours we lay there, wrist neatly slit open—I can't even find the scar—while they caught you and lost you, caught you and lost you, and then, more or less sure, caught you again (but didn't).

And now one finger doesn't work so well. I can't make a fist with my left hand, and it's hard to pick up change. (I'm left-handed, of course.) It would have to be my favorite hand that I pushed through the door glass (one drink too many).

But how I slept, truth serum in my veins, happily missing the glitter and click of hemostats. And woke to your hard professional slaps in the face, in Recovery, nurse. You must have been late for your date, good-looking nurse; your make-up was perfect when I saw you at last, and you had stopped bawling my name in my ear, like a character in *Alice in Wonderland*, stopped letting me have the flat of your hand.

Arm in sling, hand in aluminum brace, I lecture and teach while the tendon sleeps. It's not worth fixing really. I'm not a pianist or, as you put it, doctor, a Swiss watchmaker. But a dancer one night says to me at a party: Are you disfigured? (Only a dancer would use a word like that.)

Third Class, *Queen Mary*

Third Class, *Queen Mary*, late December on the high Atlantic.
    The storm is fabulous. Seas run to the height of the
    promenade deck where picture windows are smashed.
    The ocean frowns like elephant hide and has a texture
    almost smooth. In the dining room I am sat with Miss
    Cohen at a table for two. (The English keep races to-
    gether.) I tell her proudly that this was my troopship.
    Proudly I describe the Mary in wartime: gray from
    stem to stern, all ports and windows blacked, the mon-
    ster zigzagging from Boston to the Sydney Heads.
    Forty days and forty nights, Key West, Rio, Cape-
    town, south almost to Little America, north to New
    South Wales. Now it seems quiet and empty, clean and
    well-kept as a cemetery, even in this great storm.—Ah,
    this is different, says Miss Cohen: we are paying for
    this.

We are paying for this!

The server is polite and clean. He tends us in the mighty empty
    ship. The tablecloth is white, the silver silver. The
    waiters call me Sir. This voyage I am Sir. I pay.

In the vulgarity of poetic justice, Miss Cohen is knocked from
    her chair by a skyscraper sea. I visit her in the hospital.
    She is ugly; I like her. I say to myself, she offended the
    god of the storm.

Autumn reminds me

Autumn reminds me that you bit my lips, excellent nurse of the
most famous hospital, with puffy eyes and advertisable
rear. North of beautiful Baltimore, in valley taverns,
reminiscent of imagined England, we watched from
the rail fence the blessing of hounds. At the place of
our date you made a pass at my just-married friend in
the face of his bride. She is dark and full, a Renoir
woman with Brooklyn accent. You are light and thin,
lacking in humor or observation. How slowly the dark
one moves while you engage her husband in jokes and
hugs and public thigh-pushes, all thoroughly insincere.
Till the bride's laughter congeals in her throat and
suddenly she is flying hands and knives of fingernails
slashing wickedly at your soft attractive face, your
sleepless eyes with albino lashes.

At night in the improvised bed by the living-room fire in the
stone cottage you bite and use your nails. Afterwards
you want me to stay inside you the entire night, even
asleep. I laugh, I beg. Instead of whispering *darling*
you whisper (with such conviction) —*you worm!*

Priests and Freudians will understand

Priests and Freudians will understand. In the throttling Papuan
heat, even the rain is hot, even the rain carries the rot
smell. Lying in mud or in soaked hammocks the soldiers stew and joke and empty their dead minds. De-
prived of love and letters and the sight of woman, the
dead mind rots.

Who sent this missal soft and black, with iridescent gold and
five silk ribbons sewn in the binding: red, silver, blue,
green, purple? Two thousand pages mica-thin, like two
millennia of daily shame.

Nearby, the natives make themselves strong by drinking sweat
of warriors, eating fingernails coated with human
blood. Priests and Freudians comprehend. And now I
learn the missal prayers. I set up mental prayer wheels
and spin them with the whips of fear. Help me, Freudians and priests: when I say the proud Hail Mary,
the serpent takes me in the groin.

I seek the chaplain in his tent. Father, convert me. He looks
at me and says: You must excuse me, sergeant. I have
a furlough coming up.

When I say the Hail Mary I get an erection. Doesn't that
prove the existence of God?

Next to my office

Next to my office where I edit poems ("Can poems be edited?")
there is the Chicago Models Club. All day the girls
stroll past my door where I am editing poems, behind
my head a signed photograph of Rupert Brooke, hand-
somer than any movie star. I edit, keeping one eye
peeled for the models, straining my ears to hear what
they say. In there they photograph the girls on the
bamboo furniture, glossies for the pulsing façades of
night spots. One day the manager brings me flowers,
a huge and damaged bouquet: hurt gladiolas, overly
open roses, long-leaping ferns (least hurt), and bruised
carnations. I accept the gift, remainder of last night's
opening (where?), debut of lower-class blondes. I
distribute the flowers in the other poetry rooms, too
formal-looking for our disarray.

Now after every model's bow to the footlights the manager
brings more flowers, hurt gladiolas, overly open roses,
long-leaping ferns and bruised carnations. I edit poems
to the click of sharp high heels, flanked by the swords
of lavender debut, whiffing the cinnamon of crepe-
paper-pink carnations of the bruised and lower-class
blondes.

Behind me rears my wall of books, most formidable of human
barriers. No flower depresses me like the iris but these
I have a fondness for. They bring stale memories over
the threshold of the street. They bring the night of
cloth palm trees and soft plastic leopard chairs, night
of sticky drinks, the shining rhinestone hour in the
dark-blue mirror, the peroxide chat of models and
photogenic morn.

Today the manager brings all gladioli. A few rose petals lie in
the corridor. The mail is heavy this morning.

August Saturday night

August Saturday night on the Negro street the trolleys clang
and break sweet dusty smoke. Cars hoot meaningless
signals. The air is in a sweat of Jim Crow gaiety, shop-
ping, milling, rubbing of flesh, five miles of laughter
in white Baltimore. The second floor dance hall has a
famous trumpet. You can't move on the floor, which
rolls like waves and is in actual danger of giving way.
The temperature adds to the frenzy. There is no pause
in the jump and scream of the jazz, heat waves of
laughter, untranslatable slang. The dancing is de-
montic, terpsichorean. It's like a war of pleasure. It's
the joy of work. The fatigue is its own reward.

Across the street in the corner drug store where whiskey is
sold and every blandishment of skin, a teeming Negress
crowds at the perfume counter, big arms like haunches
and bosom practically bare. She laughs with her
friends above the cut-glass bottles with Frenchified
names and recently invented colors. She purchases a
sizeable vial of some green scent, pays green dry
money, unstoppers the bottle and dumps the entire
load between her breasts! O glorious act of laughter in
the half-serious bazaar of the Jew-store!

I perform in the drug-store window

I perform in the drug-store window, stretching into neatly
folded draperies the rubbery and lavender crepe paper.
Two little children watch as I empty a box of tacks
into my mouth and tread softly between two huge glass
vessels, one filled with blue water, one filled with red.
The tack hammer is magnetized. I put it to my lips
and catch a tack, point outward, swiftly fastening the
flimsy drapes this way and that. Rosettes I make,
flounces, valance at the top, then set the beautiful
cardboard actress up, life-size face selling perfume or
soap. My eyes dizzily graze her eyes.

In hardware windows comic displays of insecticides. In a thousand neighborhood bars I fashion crinkly curtains of
red to frame vast mirrors. Always a jocular free beer,
warming off-color jokes with the woman. Bars for
workingmen. I am almost a workingman I tell myself.

I am a worker I tell myself. Ils sont dans le vrai (for I am
literary). My uneasiness with salesmen, terror of the
rich. I have seven vocabularies: they change with the
locale. The city itself changes: here it is London, here
it is Paris; here it is eighteenth-century. I haunt the
second-hand bookshops or visit a one-dollar woman.
It's a tossup.

One by one my troops desert

One by one my troops desert. A hair at a time. One by one and there is no return. Yesterday it was dark and soft, unnoticeable as a pore. Today it sticks up at a crazy angle, bristling with what act of rebellion. Yesterday a tendril, a decoration, a vestige of biology, today barbed wire. I count them all till I've lost count. I count from the top of my head. The revolution started in that sector.

In the sole world of the self that is how it happens. One cell revolts against the general harmony. The body's bourgeois security is threatened. The government gives a perceptible shudder. One cell alone goes off, giving the finger sign of obscenity. Urchins and panhandlers cheer him on. In a moment he is making speeches. Then the police, then the militia, soon the victorious grave.

Rising crooked on my arm, darting wickedly out of my eyebrows, blanching my chest like sun, what do you want, blackmailers, professional mourners. I see you starting down my arms like lice, infiltrating to the very wrist. How far will you go? When will order be restored. Halfway measures for fops and actors, black dye, tweezers, cuticle scissors. Shall I give you away? I know your little game. I saw it in the bath the other day. This plot would tickle Rabelais. A pubic hair turned silver gray!

The Bach *Partitas* saved my life

The Bach *Partitas* saved my life. Floating in fever over Cincinnati, I felt the soft piano hammers sounding my chest, my soul, my balls. Ancient and skillful fingers worked their way—genius of chiropractic, I am uncracked again! Crucified on silk rope ladders that tickle the back of my neck I sail down blazing sea lanes with old poems that disgust me nowadays. I'm not sick enough for a reconciliation. Maybe I'm only malingering. The doctor says through a brandy snifter as big as my head: the virus yes, but somebody is bothering you. He's telling my fortune.

Waves of activity spring from the phonograph: the left-hand figure is deep in my bowels. Yes, there's a student wrecking my work. I'm too much of a coward to kick him out. There's a girl who was burned in a fire; I fear for her sanity. Or a Quaker lady bound for jail; and a jazz musician. I've lost the clue for keeping them together.

They used to call it brain fever or broken heart. Medicine was metaphorical in those days. But one can train a deadly disease to run your affairs while you're away. You adopt it while it is young, shower it with affection, give it the confidence of education.

Stay in bed for a week. Learn the *Partitas*. This music forgives me. Love of simplicity, fear of the obvious, at bottom the dread of being an impostor. Is it ever too late to denounce? The music is playing me—the wrong approach as usual.

Mr. Cochran flags the train

Mr. Cochran flags the train. One man with a flag can stop all that steam and steel and make it roll again. He sits in a doll house by the railroad track and we go there to keep him company. All day he whittles and tells us stories. He whittles us fine sticks with designs. His favorite pattern is pitting with an awl. A stick of wood becomes a talisman with stars, indentations, smooth and magical. When we go home for our nap we show our treasures.

Two Boy Scouts climb the switch tower to pay a visit to Mr. Carter. He sits at rows of lights and black-handled levers, dangerous to touch. Everything up here is dangerous and thrilling. Mr. Carter whittles people, naked people with private parts. Sometimes there are two people stuck together in crazy positions. It's quite a museum up here. When the lift-gates clang and drop and the traffic piles up, we all look down on the open automobiles, girls in bathing suits going to the beach. The tower trembles with the thunder of the freight train.

This figurine of steatite speaks to me. Narrow eyes, thick lips, flat nose, deep carven beard and hair, deep clover-pattern of vestment. Chalcolithic of Mohenjo-Daro.

In the junk shop I ask to buy the life-size wooden horse. It came from a saddler's of the sod-house days. But it's not for sale except to a museum. We go away, my daughter and I, with a milking stool, nice near the fireplace.

Every day when I walk by

Every day when I walk by the immense publishing company,
I know they are rolling out enormous medical tomes.
And I know, like a secret, they are printing my book
of poems. In front of the rounded plate-glass windows
I am Raskolnikov. Yet I don't affront the editor: it's
purely a business transaction to him.

I want the title page just so. I show a D. H. Lawrence title
page, boldface British, unmistakable. The rest in book
type, untechnological. The conventional length of
sixty-four pages, poetry-size. The binding maroon.

In gold I also use my middle initial but spelled out JAY. J is
for Jacob. My father dropped his first name Israel. My
son is named Jacob. Upper-class Jews call him Jack.
My father-in-law's name was Jack, probably Jacob.

The act of a book to hold in the hand is its own reason. The
little defiance of a book of poems. Bludgeoning and
recompense of uncles.

I said to Ignotus

I said to Ignotus in the shadow of the peristyle: I will carry
your message *to take the side of the child forever*. And
I stood on the banks of the Ohio River and I used cunning and loud-mouth. There I rocked the solid Dagons
on the block-letter pedestals and they crashed down on
the city (I think). And I sat by the golf course and
drank Scotch and in one afternoon evoked a new god.
And graybeards milled at the corners with sullenness.
Doors of reformatories flew open. Red lights were
hung at the porches of churches. And I wept for
clowns. And a female secretary at a publisher's office
asked to be arrested. And a famous scholar lunged at
my face with a desk spindle. And thus we proclaimed
Christmas on earth, Ignotus.

These things take time, or an earthquake. People are reluctant
to relinquish their holdings in libraries. The children
themselves are unreliable: why shouldn't they be sus-
picious. Their hiding places are known by the international police. Their telephone wires are cut at the
drop of a hat. In every closet the hooded sisters and
the reversible fathers. It's that or the doctor boiling his
knives. There's one good thing about the culture gods:
they're fresh out of poison (I think). Unless they're
planning our final Fourth of July. They have a place
to go. They always do.

Your book about my books

Your book about my books, which I'm the only reader of. O
   book that's absolutely mine, that I didn't have a hand
   in. Mirror of my Narcissus years, music box, what if I
   stop now? List of notices that brought me nights of
   delirium, ecstasy, fury, heartbreak, mirror broken and
   magically joined together without a flaw. History of
   me which only I can read. And you, my author, what
   thanks or regrets shall I give? You took me alive,
   hands tied behind, delivered me to the marshal of
   degrees. There on the platform where all things fall
   through, I went down in operatic flames. In velvet
   cape and sword of pen, I accepted.

Incapacity for sincerity reminds me of an oral question:
   Molière, était-il sincère? (What in the name of God is
   prose?)

Phone book of myself, I will call you up.

French poetry

French poetry that always goes itself one better.

French poetry of figure 5's and rust carnations.

French poetry of the tongue that tastes of women and children, spatulas and rubber plants.

French poetry of the tiniest print to be read with bifocals when snow first enters the rain with its wicked announcements of defeat.

French poetry of marginal headaches, wood fires, cold, sixteen-millimeter surrealist films, Martinique jazz and the woman across the way, utmost gravity and indestructible balance, winner of the double medallion,

Easter Island images, the monstrous solemnity of patriotic children and ribbons.

French poetry of convenience, Satanism, baroque brass keys to hospitals, and cats.

French poetry of the line drawn with the fist on the pale nuance,

Overly cultivated snows, sick castles.

French poetry of the exquisite ruins of conversation.

French poetry that upsets the stomach of the future.

Of frockless priests, glorious geometricians, child insurrectionists.

French poetry of the Statue of Liberty, battered by kisses
and dentists,

Ropy veins of the feet of matrons and whores, stigmata, épée.

French poetry of the Missouri River, the Platte, Yarra, gutter
water of the rue Jacob.

Gloire, Vrai, et cetera.

What kind of notation is in my *Time* file

What kind of notation is in my *Time* file for my life, especially
my death? Will they say I died, O God? If they don't
say I died how can I die? There it is fine and relevant
to die, an honor so to speak, interesting as divorce.

What's in my file at the F.B.I.? What's my symbol when they
flick me out? Am I a good American or a borderline
case? Can I hold my liquor? Have I ever been cleared,
and if so, of what?

Dear Fame, I meet you in the damnedest places. You smile,
you walleyed bitch, but you look over my shoulder for
a prearranged signal: something has come up on the
other side of the room.

My life, my own, who is writing you on what pale punch
cards? Deep-thinking machine, have you got my number?

A hundred oligarchs in identical suits are sitting around a
table shaped like a uterus, alphabetizing greatness. I
say to myself: all men are great. I would like to cry
but have forgotten how. Now I remember: they used
to come to me, those journalists with humble pencils.
They begged me from their hats: say something big;
give us an execution; make bad weather. I failed them
badly. I couldn't grow a beard.

I guess I haven't built my ship of death. The word "image" is
now in government. The doors are all closing by remote control. But when I meet the almighty Publicity
Director, name-dropper of kings, I'll shake his hand

and say: once I kissed Fame (mouth like an ass hole) but only for fun. He'll tear up the punch cards and think for a minute.

As you say (not without sadness),
poets don't see, they feel

As you say (not without sadness), poets don't see, they feel.
And that's why people who have turned to feelers seem
like poets. Why children seem poetic. Why when the
sap rises in the adolescent heart the young write
poetry. Why great catastrophes are stated in verse.
Why lunatics are named for the moon. Yet poetry isn't
feeling with the hands. A poem is not a kiss. Poems
are what ideas feel like. Ideas on Sunday, thoughts on
vacation.

Poets don't see, they feel. They are conductors of the senses
of men, as teachers and preachers are the insulators.
The poets go up and feel the insulators. Now and
again they feel the wrong thing and are thrown
through a wall by a million-volt shock. All insulation
makes the poet anxious: clothes, strait jackets, imabic
five. He pulls at the seams like a boy whose trousers
are cutting him in half. Poets think along the electric
currents. The words are constantly not making sense
when he reads. He flunks economics, logic, history.
Then he describes what it feels like to flunk economics,
logic, history. After that he feels better.

People say: it is sad to see a grown man feeling his way, sad
to see a man so naked, desireless of any defenses. The
people walk back into their boxes and triple-lock
the doors. When their children begin to read poetry the
parents watch them from the corner of their eye. It's
only a phase, they aver. Parents like the word "aver"
though they don't use it.

Randall, I like your poetry terribly

Randall, I like your poetry terribly, yet I'm afraid to say so.
Not that my praise keeps you awake—though I'm
afraid it does. I can't help liking them. I even like the
whine, the make-believe whiplash with the actual wire
in it. Once when you reviewed me badly (you must)
I wrote you: "I felt as if I had been run over but not
hurt." That made you laugh. I was happy. It wasn't
much of a triumph but it worked. When people ask
about you I am inclined to say: He's an assassin (a
word I never use). I'm inclined to say: Why are you
always yourself? Your love of Rilke—if it's love—
your intimacy with German and God knows what all,
your tenderness and terrorization, your prose sentences
—like Bernini graves, staggeringly expensive, Ital-
ianate, warm, sentences once-and-for-all. And the
verses you leave half-finished in mid-air—I once knew
a woman who never finished a sentence. Your mind is
always at its best, your craft the finest craft "money
can buy" you would say with a barb. I'm afraid of
you. Who wouldn't be. But I rush to read you, whatever you print. That's news.

They held a celebration for you

They held a celebration for you, Charles, in Iowa. I was asked
but I regretted. It was the hundredth birthday of your
book, your proper Christian book called *Flowers of
Evil*. (Or is it THE *Flowers of Evil*? I never know.)
And in that hymnal, how well you made yourself in
the image of Poe—Poe with a cross, that's what you
are, adored of the gangster age. In fact, aren't you a
children's poet? Aren't you the Lewis Carroll of small
vice? Your shabby Wonderland of pus and giant
nipple, your cats and jewels and cheap perfumes, your
licking Lesbians and make-believe Black Mass, O
purulence of Original Sin. And always playing it safe
in the end, like Disneyland. So many safety devices,
pulleys, cranks, classical Alexandrines. It's Iowa for
you, restless spirit, where elderly ladies embezzle millions in the *acte gratuite*. You'll need no naturaliza-
tion papers here. And yet I loved you once, and
Delacroix and Berlioz—all in my gangster age. The
little boy in me loved you all, O solemn Charles, so
photogenic. And this is my flower for your anniver-
sary. I fashioned it of Mexican tin and black nail
polish, little French Swinburne burning in Iowa City.

Each in her well-lighted picture window

Each in her well-lighted picture window, reading a book or
magazine, the Amsterdam whores look quite domestic.
The canals, as picturesque as expected, add their
serenity. The customers stroll from window to window, back and forth, comparing merchandise. Where
a curtain is drawn, business is being transacted. These
are big, fine, strapping whores, heavy in the leg, blond,
as is the preference. They don't display their wares, no
more than crossing a leg. It's like a picture gallery,
Flemish School, silent through varnish and glaze.
What detail, what realism of texture, what narrative!
And look at this masterpiece:

A solid blond sits in her window at an angle. She appears to
be looking out, expressionless. Just back of her stands
an African king in round white hat and lengthy white
embroidered robe of satin, it may be. Behind him
stands his servant, very straight. The king's face is a
thin and noble ebony. And without looking at either
African the whore holds one hand back of her shoulder, feeling the robe of the African king with eloquent
fingers, weighing the heft of the silk in her thoughtful
hand.

I drove three thousand miles to ask a question

I drove three thousand miles to ask a question. No answer,
naturally. It served me right; I'm not the pilgrim type.
I wanted a first-hand account of *him*: when he was
alive, before they murdered him. When you worked
with him, before they drove him insane, I laughed
like the others. I said: My friend, you swim among the
blues of the lunatic fringe as always. This is only
another of your voyages. But did you leave him before
he died or after? Did you go to the trial? Were you
there when the police smashed the equipment? Did you
visit him in the sunset of his mind?

In the soft San Diego sunset you turned your back. I don't
want to talk about that, you said. Your little dogs
leaped up at me with teeth. Our children ran wild together. Your wife sang beautifully. In the morning
you cashed me a check, arriving at the bank in a
foreign car.

Did you really recover from the death of your father? I must
hear about the other from someone I know as well as
you. You are the only one. We didn't get along was
all you said. I don't want to discuss him. The disciples
are scattered. They are all in hiding. It's against the
law to post his books. Everyone seems ashamed for a
different reason. Is his wife living, his child? Where
is truth's underground? How long does love stay murdered? Did he have to sentence himself? The lab ex-
periment of his life is proved—there must have been
another way. Pictures that he took when the bulbs
popped, each brighter than a thousand suns; the spiral
poems he wrote under the electronic microscope—mad
scientist, good German—fixed in my mind and locked
in yours.

The day you discover

The day you discover that your favorite poet is a homosexual,
and the heated argument dies down after an hour, and
you have lost, you are like a prince who has been
brought bad tidings and you sit with an empty belly
while they take the messenger out of the room to be
shot. Tomorrow it will be different but tonight you
feel an impersonal sorrow as nagging as envy. When
later you read his poems, with another dimension
added to their music, they will seem more distant, like
fine translations. A dry wash of the face will suffice
for your pleasure. It's not the same as with Shakespeare or the plain Cavafy. You can shrug at the
Greeks and the Bulgarians. But this is a secret that
had to be told to be known.

Close the door of your mind on those love letters. Beware of
the poison of pronouns. Suddenly you are coarse with
limitation, gruff before flowers, your own poems
lumpy, indelicate. The it-ness of trees! And Emily
too? And the brotherhood of man—is that one? Peni-
tentiaries, navies, hospitals, football teams! Where
will it end?

Poet who lies with the sea, dancer who shrugs one shoulder,
lecturer with the turquoise ring, exquisite conversa-
tionalist, you with the beard and the lake-water eyes,
woman with the voice of woodwinds—why do you slap
me? Is there a poetry where what happens in bed is
lucky on the page and the poem is actually for her?

Why am I happy writing this textbook

Why am I happy writing this textbook? What sublime idiocy! What a waste of time! A textbook on prosody at that. Yet when I sit down to comb the business out, when I address the easel of this task, I burn with an even flame, I'm cooking with gas. There are some things so dull they hypnotize like the pendulum of a clock; so clockwork and quotidian they make the flesh delirious like fresh water. X-ray the poem, give it a thorough physical, a clean bill of health. We can see everything but the flow of blood. What Latin and Greek nomenclature! But this is order, order made to order. This is system to plot and plan. This is definition, edges clean as razors. Simplification, boldface, indented. I know there is no such thing as a textbook. I know that all textbooks are sold the second the course is over. I know that a book sold is a dead book. And I dream, like others, of writing a textbook that is not a textbook, a book that not even a student would part with, a book that makes even prosody breathe. So, when the sun shines with the nine o'clock brightness and the coffee swims in my throat and the smoke floats over the page like the smoke of a ship's funnel, then I romanticize. I make a muse of prosody, old hag. She's just a registered nurse, I know, I know, but I have her sashay, grind and bump, register Alcaics, Sapphics, choriambs (my predilection). She's trained all right. She's second nature herself. She knows her job, I mine. We'll work it out: it may be poetry. Blueprints are blue. They have their dreams.

They erect a bust of me after my death

They erect a bust of me after my death. I know the right
alcove, where the students sit, in the library corridor,
smoking and joking about the professors. "I fought
with tooth and nail to save my niche."

A bust in the modern mode, more than slightly abstract, in a
dull metal perhaps, of the new alloys I love. No lapis
lazuli "big as a Jew's head cut off at the nape." I wish
I had a leonine head, the kind to start a sculptor's
fingers twitching.

There was a bust of me a student made, life-size and a good
likeness, age twenty-one when I wore a pompadour.
In plaster it was much too white. We painted it green,
then pink, then black, then sandpapered it down and
called it Scrofula. One night we stuck it in a mound
of dirt outside where they were mending the street.
That was the end of it. Baltimore has too many monuments already.

Baltimore has Poe and also Lanier. Lizette Reese and Francis
Scott Key. Baltimore has poets and poets. —Which
uncle put the money up?

Posterity is a literary racket

Posterity is a literary racket. Posterity is a switchboard to past, present, and future. Posterity is an intercom system devised by the brain of super-educationalists in faraway almost nonexistent places like offices. Posterity lives in the vaults of the nearest insurance company. Posterity is for the fabulously rich. The poor plant potatoes in the bathtub and dandle their children and listen to beery poetry on broken sofas.

The term *generation* is a deadly weapon. When a poet says "my generation," move off a few feet. He probably has a switch-blade knife up his sleeve, and it's for "my" generation. If you want to join the poet's army, just give the password: my generation. Generations are organizations, like General Motors. Posterity is a de facto government of clean-jawed men with high ideals and two telephones in every bathroom. It's always the generation that takes the credit for whatever is credited. Always posterity that catches the hell of the last generation. Posterity lies in wait for the innocent, a monstrous grave to swallow the grandchildren, dug by the lean-jawed voices of ideals. A source close to posterity tells me that this generation isn't going well and may have to take its place in the catacombs.

God couldn't stand the sight of Cain

God couldn't stand the sight of Cain. Nor could he stand the
flowing rows of wheat and the sweet rye grass as green
as a garden. The smoke flew back in the face of Cain
and choked him. Abel wept. Abel was afraid of his
brother and went for a walk in the open country. The
jealousy of God sat heavily on Cain. He killed his
younger brother with a stone. It might have been
worse, much worse. Then Cain's own children, for-
bidden their land, invented cities and the culture of
cities. But God hated cities as fast as they were built.
And the cities were never really on His side. The
cities grew bigger, the women more beautiful, and
God more angry.

The fish are exempt for some reason

The fish are exempt for some reason. The waters of the abyss
wash everything clean. Now the animals are scamper-
ing down the mountainside headed for the swimming
jungles. The patriarch and his family move in awe on
the mountain, under the sky of broken clouds where
the sun pours through and the rainbow bends its
colors. They sing, they pray like pilgrims from over
the sea. God has regained his temper. The murders
of Cain and Lamech are over and done with. But
shortly Noah harvests the grapes and gets thoroughly
drunk. Lying nude and erect on his bed he is found
by his son. This constitutes a crime and the son is
cursed forever. It's the ritual of shame enforced by
God. The patriarch destroys the son because of his
own unconscious natural lust. (The other brothers
backed into the tent, so as not to see the holy object,
and covered it with a blanket. For which they were
richly rewarded.)

What the analyst said

What the analyst said when he came from the exhibit (he
      was rather drunk) amounted to this: A clean white
      wall in an uncluttered room is the ground. You take
      a clean white wall and hang a rock, a sock, a split of
      log, a bag of dreck—give it the frame of a clean white
      wall, and that's abstract.

I looked around the clean white room. Schwitters fritterings
      of old bus tickets, gracefully mounted bit on bit, for
      fade of color, take of depth, alone on its panel. Bronze
      drip of narrow stems of bronze Giocometti; teakwood
      base. Enormous almost idiot head of Christ, hydro-
      cephalic, brushed in dusty yellows. A female thigh,
      reddish close-grained jarrah wood, with a high polish.

I love abandoned barns weathered to silver, the drip of rust
      from reinforcement iron stars on old American brick;
      driftwood of course; objects found to hand; fondling-
      stones; packets of Japanese black pebbles; shards; un-
      dressed planking; ax marks on a fashionable mantle,
      twelve by twelve; pock-marked travertine; rose-red
      hinges; ten-cent-store utensils; comic strips with paren-
      theses denoting frustration or beating wings; Samuel
      Greenberg and Rupert Brooke.

The preacher

The preacher (say Episcopal) alone on a lone day (Tuesday perhaps, off season for great holidays) in his fine small church (not small if you are in it long enough), really in solitude in the minor splendor. One supposes he has finished his chores, whatever they are, and is returning the absorption of the stage-lit solitude. Nevertheless everything is present, with objects having taken on the quality of human beings. He's not what you would call a contemplative. He snatches time like a schoolteacher, or waits for it, miserly, knowing that it will come with interest. And when it comes (which is rather more often than anyone expects, or even wants), his first sensation is collapse, his second to sit where the Sunday people pray. There, though it has the musk of a railroad station (not really), he takes a seat for a moment, gets up, sits down. He is one of them now, in the back of his head. The hedges are such a brown that spring is about to thorn on the world-side of the purple glass with its legends so strictly ruled on the calendar. He has no grief. This paperwork of saving souls! Could there be quiet in the stolen moment, moment of fame with God. But everything stirs, even though noiselessly. Could there be thoughts that turn to stone after the hammering, forever. O leaves of stone, come forth in a cool summering of prayer and change my spirit into a fine small church on the world's quietest street. My hands of vellum folded, I could pray.

I'm writing this poem for someone to see

I'm writing this poem for someone to see when I'm not looking.
     This is an open book. I want to be careful to startle
     you gently. The poem is about your looking at it, as
     one looks at a woman covertly. (I wonder what she's
     doing in this town; it's a long way from the look in her
     eyes.) The rings of my big notebook stand open like
     the rib cage of a baracuda. Careful with your fingers.

I'm writing this poem for an after-dinner friend who's using
     my pipe tobacco or my pen. I'd like some phrase to
     catch his eye. I'd like some phrase to wake him up in
     the early hours, as one wakes up with a fragment of
     tune in his head (the melody for the day). The toilet
     bowls glow graciously and there's a box of the best
     Kleenex on the sink. I'm writing this poem for hos-
     pitality. I can't stand people who say Help Yourself.
     That always means Don't Be a Pig. Tired of picking
     the locks of poems I leave this one for all and sundry.
     To put your name in it would be a dirty trick.

Younger I dreamed of being a poet whose trash basket was
     rifled by scholars. I learned to write trash-basket
     poems. But this is closer to my real desire. I'm writing
     this poem as much for you as a poem is possible. It
     stands there like a half-filled glass, both coming and
     going. I'm a bad host. The drinks are too strong; I
     don't know how to carve (I say with a grin, I'm left-
     handed). This is a poem to sneak at a glance. (I'm
     writing it to mean, not be.)

In a flash I see my mistake

In a flash I see my mistake and put it out of my mind. But I'm
through tearing out my marginalia, erasing my notes
and drunken commentaries. "The man writes prose
like a lunatic." By the time I run across this again I
am praising his prose and getting it published. Here's
an old poem that loves Eliot. I outline the Zohar, especially the glyph of the Tree of Life. It's a long way
around to the truth that you started with. Belief is the
greatest tragedy of man. Only the heroes walk through
life not even aware of belief. Lunatics! Saints!

When Tertullian died the angels jumped out of their nightgowns and went at it like goats. Any belief, the more
far-fetched the better, can explain everything. It is
diseased to believe. Now it's old Tolstoy who has me
by the short hairs and hisses *hate Shakespeare*. I hate
him for a lecture or two. Then I hate Leo. Then I'm
back to normal. As for the errors, think nothing of
them. Somebody fools you every day of your life.
Track down the jokers and nail them flat. Never mind
backtracks. Don't look behind you. And if anybody
asks you: never apologize, even to God.

Cat called me a Jewish pig

Cat called me a Jewish pig. Cat said to me in a voice so normal
    she might be ordering ham from a yard-high menu:
    You are the most insensitive man I've ever met.

Cat and I were walking down the Cathouse street off Bug-
    house Square in Chicago. Her husband was trying to
    lose us (you can hardly blame him). Where is your
    lovely husband, Cat? She wheeled around and pointed
    through the neon baleful glare: There comes the little
    fucker, that little black thing two inches high.

She sulked on a sofa in a shabby dress, looking like an Irish
    maid on her day off in the walnut-paneled living room.
    She seethed with worms at so much rich stupidity.
    Hell flowed from her mouth like streams of horse,
    splashing the blue Picassos.

For breakfast we have beer. Where the scum of fame backed
    up in the estuary Cat bathed with hopeless soap. The
    sky grew dingier than pans. In the vomit of news she
    spun like a carousel and fell through sobs to the drome-
    dary dolls.

Cat went walking through the slaughterhouse where the prime
    hogs dance on the end of a chain and the throats are
    slit to empty the black blood. She groaned in the
    screaming of pork and was given perfume.

Cat left her laundry and forgot to get it. Five miles in the air
    you could hear her scream of love. At the soup kitchen
    of poets she gloomed like a sphinx. She stroked the
    oxygen tank like a bomb with a name. She exhausted
    the language of blame. With the dry shrapnel of love

she shaved her head in the gleaming sleet of literature.
Her typewriter keys were tipped with tetanus praise.
She cursed the cyclamen, good Saint Cat.

He said it: Kill the poet in yourself

He said it: Kill the poet in yourself. He said it well. Now he is
surrounded by juries in every direction. Whole pas-
sages are read by the court clerk; the women bow their
heads as if in prayer. Some have never even heard
the words that kill. The men are always angriest or
aggrieved. I think: the pig is taboo to the Jews because
it was once their god. Are those words gods? The
people want their poetry of not saying, don't touch,
hold your shoulders straight. They turn the book in
their hands like a time bomb. Something goes off in
their laps but no one is frightened. Much talk of taking
a bath. A bidet is brought for exhibit. Demonstrations.
Laughter. Waving of state flags. No one is certain
precisely what the issue is. The testimony grows
learned; big words are rolled in like balls of dung.
Why are the edges of the Bible red not blue? I think
we are losing. The experts falter. Housewives examine
their fingernails: this is the end. The hilarious thing is
the way he sides with the judges, like Jesus. The veil
is rent by a tremendous blat. Dogs cry in their sleep.
Children playing doctor are hustled off to the federal
prisons. The wife of the President crosses herself before releasing the bottle of champagne against the lead
wall of the fall-out shelter. The judge is clutching the
Good. Nobody knows what happened to the True. The
Beautiful has fainted dead away (she has her instruc-
tions).

Dylan wasn't dapper

Dylan wasn't dapper. Uncle Saul was a dandy. Dylan stole and
borrowed. Uncle Saul likewise. Dylan stole a shirt or
two and some bottles of whiskey. Uncle Saul purloined
whole wardrobes, used checking accounts that didn't
belong to him, charged at the best shops under others'
names. Dylan wore motley, Uncle Saul silk. Dylan
was short and curly. Uncle Saul wore Cuban heels to
raise himself and ordered Scotch in the barber's chair.
Dylan played at pinballs. Uncle won the monthly rent
at poker or bridge. Dylan borrowed women. Uncle
Saul hired them and kept them in love nests. Dylan's
look was straight and far into your eyes. The eyes of
Uncle Saul were always merry and shrewd but you
couldn't see beyond their twinkle and scheme. Dylan
was a civilian. Uncle wangled a commission in the
Army, only to be discharged for juggling money
records. Uncle Saul kept the table choking with
laughter and sang falsetto and clowned in a lavender
dressing gown, with masses of hair on his chest. Dylan
toured America like a favorite nephew, sprinkling
dynamite on the nipples of female professors. He had
the discipline of a lovely knave.

Now both are dead, Dylan and Uncle Saul. Dylan was taken
by the pickling of his beautiful brain. The sacred
oxygen could not reach the convolutions. Uncle Saul
was taken thrice by the heart, thrice by the broken
personality. Uncle Saul joked in the lobby of the plush
nuthouse, wearing a brilliant sportcoat and shined elegant shoes. The black hair dye had vanished; his hair
was snowy white. They gave him the shock treatment
until his heart exploded. Dylan lay inert with the

Moses bumps on his forehead amidst the screaming of wives and the groans of lovers and drinkers. And the Beat said—iambic killed him.

Glottal as a bottle, everybody loves you

Glottal as a bottle, everybody loves you, only you don't believe
it. Hulk of greenery among the desert great, your roots
grab continents of sham and groan. You masticate all
dictionaries and spew out one-word spitballs on the
walls. You blackboard buccaneers of blah. You housel
planetaria of spurt. You shoeshine flesh with hail and
hurt. Psychologically, you sport.

The music flutes: you're nursing Mother Goose. You know
her nasty secrets like a name (dirty old woman stinking of gin). Have you found the pickled foetuses! Does
your poem purl in Polish? Who's bigger than you—
those squishy dreams?

The decencies file in: such pretty girls, such beardy boys.
Your rhythms that throb like ocean motors.

Now and then the darkness of stanzas. That bridge of ice-
capped sawtooth monuments bites at the sky like in-
dustrial diamonds. You grit your teeth on broken glass,
sing with a geographical tongue on the sly nights of
Seattle. Art is a blood pudding foreign as frescoes.
Where you dig down we are, we are. Under the smoky
glass we are. How the flukes splash, ha-ha, baby!

When they ask about your poems

When they ask about your poems I say: He writes like a truck
driver (if only you did). Your idiom coarse as Indian
hair, you click along on Union Pacific meters. You tell
your rhymes like beads; you ambiguate as well as the
gobbledegooks. Honor bright. We all came out of the
same army and joined the same generation of silence.
Each took the territory of his choice (yours is the
biggest). You handle Dante like a Cadillac. (Our
colleague drives a Mercedes-Rilke. Our serious one
can't tell the names of cars.) Good social conscience,
lover of gab and gag, you're known in every dimension, heart like a halfback—

One time you beaned the lady-poet, I scratched my head.
What the hell were you trying to do? People attack
affinities. The gurus call you middlebrow; you shrug it
off. You feel at home in the poetry lab, a manual or two
under your belt. This isn't an ad or a tax return. It's a
Chanukah card with Haitian angels. The Christmas
seal says Help Fight Gongorism. You weave across the
country like a trend. Have you lost the essential bum?
It's not what you sit on. The busted image has melted
back together, as hot as cooling glass. Now that the
Bishop's got his ashes hauled.

As richly documented as the hell of priests

As richly documented as the hell of priests, yes, there is a hell, the hell of sick poets, the hell of history. Those in whom honesty has turned to policy. Those diseased by notice. Those who invent new prosodies, with a logical or graphic notation. Those who wear the cold handcuffs of rhyme. Those who construct a religion of the beautiful, with symbols as the means and myth as the end. Those who mistake rage for intensity, symmetry for design, metaphor for focus, drunkenness for vision. Those who make an example of their lives and who commit acts of personal violence for public response. These inhabit the hell of poets.

Some die early by disease or accident. Some jump in the sea or drink lacerating poisons manufactured for toilets. Some lie in asylums with eyeballs metamorphosed to marble. (You cannot penetrate below their surface.) Some fall on their knees before two pieces of wood or a stone belly. Some join the revolutions and are gladly shot. Some become officials, laureates, men of affairs or major diplomats. Some become abstractionists, actuaries, mathematicians. Some become salesmen or lay priests, after their voluptuous poems are in print. Some become preachers in the last half of their lives, constructing faultless sermons. Some succumb to pageantry, some to algolagnia.

We pick some unsuspecting soul

We pick some unsuspecting soul, usually a friend, on whom
to visit a lifetime of frustration. Usually a friend, at
one fell swoop. That's what friends are for.

Incapable of loyalty, I marvel at it, imitate it nicely. But the
feeling comes from outside. It doesn't sprout in my
own soil. I carry it from a florist of sorts, some man
or woman of character, and tend it lovingly. It strug-
gles manfully in my slant sun, flourishes in the room
where I am. I scat the cat away with a loud newspaper. All my plants are exotics, bamboo, rubber,
cocoa, some with names I have never found out. They
do well in the hothouse of my eye; they bring admir-
ing glances. I sketch the shadows now and then.

At the bottom of the rubber plant one great leaf is dying an
interesting death. It dies with astonishing rapidity.
Monday, a few dabs of bright yellow. Tuesday, a
ladder of yellow on one side. Wednesday, half green,
half yellow, split down the middle. Thursday a spot
of deadly brown. Then the whole thing twists to a
Dead Sea Scroll of deadness. A single new leaf will
take a month to come.

What you say is true: I have no friends.

In the Clearing I am at peace

In the Clearing I am at peace. Place without memory or
charm. Stores practically empty of goods, schools
kindly and frightened. This Clearing is a beach without a sea.

Here there is only sporadic and symbolic violence. The clouds
are all the news. Each tree is grown by hand.

By degrees, those who have ambience are alienated from the
Dark Towers: the German groaning for the picture
galleries; the bank director who bakes his own bread;
the housewife with a flair for words who has given up
bathing; the itinerant pianist with ice-blue eyes; the
Siberian physicist with his smug compliments; the Oxford don with the dirtiest stories; the rabbi with the
mystique of the Sabbath Queen; the bearded classicist
with broken arches; the veteran bomber of three world
wars. I talk to the man who brings the firewood. He
gives me a wedge for a present.

The citizens of Nowhere scatter in all directions.

Upon my discharge from the Army my handwriting changed.
Neat slant characters gave way to square and upright.
The color of the ink no longer mattered. I met a poet
who printed all his words. (I thought this dangerous.) I find I can barely read the mail that comes.
Sometimes I have it read to me. I tend to misunder-
stand the words. My answers are brief. I still wait
for the mailman, a vestigial pleasure. Mail in the
Clearing is lighter.

Big Sonnet

Balcony Scene

You have beautiful Middle Western legs.
Widow-woman, why on Memorial Day, you who love white,
    did your bathing suit turn black? Woman in naked
    white and black. He dove down the billion-dollar
    plane, hands at the juke-box switches. The Christmas
    tree was clicking in the window. Grief I never heard.
    Your children walk on the soft excellent grass. Peonies
    lean their hairdos fatly, hands on hips.

Fatlady, I love your face, sort of slapped together. And when
    you walk (white bathing suit, black) it's as if one hip,
    the right, for instance, were going out of joint, but to
    return, a throwing motion, throwing-away, a gener-
    osity. You bend from the vertical, raising your bottom
    to the blazing sky.

Sunburn. Happy the widow with a hard white ass and a
    willow tree. O pickpock moon, subject of all lost
    poems, birthplace of tides et cetera, true bottom of the
    sea et cetera, O wallsocket.

Vacation

Goldness and whiteness of woman, like a Grand Rapids bed
    or a Sunday paper of brides. The bride coated with
    power stands in the strongest light at last. She is
    clean.—The sculptor sets his jaw and drives to the
    junk yard. There he can breathe.

Love on the deathbed, love deeper than sunset. The Bros.
    are coming. What! is it nothing but that? Is love
    nothing but that? Battle of Waterloo, nothing but
    that? Fraulein, allumeuse? Or to end a sentence with
    a preposition?

Six cases of bourbon returned to the caterer and the flowers
    divided. Hymen hymenaee.

Man with the lamp, hands of ferroconcrete, vellum of hand,
    the skin as soft as kid. Big black flashlight, size of a
    horsecock, mother's gift. Night silent as handwriting,
    night with two cats on long thin ropes. The leather
    coat of early night on the great wet lakes. Woman,
    homo normalis!

Consider also their baths, their bows, their brown blood, their
    pots, their stenches, out of which the greatest of son-
    net cycles.

Anti-Poem

Orchards hang in the newspaper of sky. It's snowing names
and addresses over the world, O lovely splash!

In dry percussion, hammers of prosperity practice against the
too-green corn. The wheat field narrows, then disappears, leaving a memory of dry wind-waves. Who
eats dry wheat but boys, wheat the hue of the backs of
eighteen-century books. Children spring from the
doors where there are no trees. Roofer up there, it's
been a good day.

On the oldest plains rise the newest houses, smelling of rose
sawdust and nails. The clammy mortar structures itself. Everyone looks like a possible Survivor. Is he
one? Is she one? Who reinvented the secret stairway,
passage to the room of Poe, chapel without a god?

Christ is in voice. The mayor is pleased with the murals. The
Jews next door are less noisy. Set the alarm for seven.

The child says: You have gray hair—you are an idiot!

The beauty is gone across the fence, the busted nose in poetry.

When I see you walk away, I love you.

When I see your back, the curves of your shoulders, your hair
the world worked on.

When I see you holding ginger by the throat.

The way a woman takes—anything (but never refuses)—is
beautiful, so to speak. The way she turns it in her
hands, holding it, not holding it. The way it catches

the light and she appraises it (in the pawnshop of her mind). Magnetism enters the thing, five minutes, eight minutes, zero minutes. She'll throw it in the trash or give it to someone she's better than. The gestures of those handsome hands.

Death of a Student

Down the funeral aisle ("my" student in coffin, car wreck, youngish death, eyeglasses polished, suit pressed as if for class, except that he's dead) come the grandparents, farmers, barely walking. Followed by yet another generation—over the arm of a younging man a girl about three asleep—drugged?—her golden pony tail flopping, asleep.

Tie tied, suit without lint, the curt sadistic sermon. Love stiffens her back. The child evades the question, as if tossing her hair. Nihilo lies sleeping.

Basement Apartment

Hymen's got a cold. Hymen, your nose is running.

My love, you look like Beethoven, like you were hit by a truck.
You look like a fucking skull.

It's six o'clock, you're drunk, you speak Greek in your sleep,
   you snore like Henry the Ninth. Wake up and take
   the dimes off my eyes.

The head of shame is red. The revenue stamp on the liquor
   bottle is red. Accidental baby, where's the Med
   School?

Trafe is the color of my true love's hair. Thank God for rain,
   blizzards, onions, and clap. Head like a broken sunflower rolling on its neck.

Coat, I place my hands in your empty pockets, thievery of
   nihilo, all the same illegal. Hands are illegal, teeth
   and tongue, books, bottles, dry rust carnations, babies,
   weeping, and law.

Two cars, one male, one female in every nest of love.

Two hearts with internal combustion engines.

Two broomsticks in every garage—ride 'em cowboy!

Bird's nest for a birthday or a sword.

Wholicity! Verset.

The Witches Are Flying

I know a man who bought a fire engine to rebuild into a twice-
life-size Stutz Bearcat. There's a man in New York
builds cars a hundred feet long so they can't turn
corners.

Big sonnet. Thing without eyes; that moves. Verset.

Letters stuck with dirt as a signature. Verset.
Byzant! Byzant! Stutz Bearcat long as a block. Glory,
glory, glory, packaged or loose, or in throwaway
bottles. Duende the darkness.

Autumn, a generation of trees gives up the ghost. Hour of
football, bituminous butterflies, vicious professors var-
nishing their desks.

Autumn, some prisoner in Iowa gives up the ghost. In bad
faith I pretend to hear the creaking of his rope in the
sole moment before his neck cracks—who has just
eaten two helpings of shortcake and asked the newspapers for our forgiveness.

Third ejaculation of the hanged man, last seed spent in the
hand of justice. Sixty-five poets cower in the poetry
shack expecting advancement.

Teamsters Union

Sorrow has moved away like happiness. The Bros. depart.

When poetry is written the trucks come. The Bros. are here. China is being packed in Cheerio cartons, the best books are wrapped in Dacron drawers. The Bros. are careful.

Great vans that smash vacationers like cockroaches, vans with names as high as windmills, noble, impersonal.

End in sight, I have your phone number. I make the nasty clicks of the dial, quickly, with the accuracy of the drum of an empty revolver. Sounds fall, like when the pussy willow goes to seed, or heady dandelions or sycamore trash balls.

Ex stasis—out of this world. Teamsters Union.

The song of the phone has quit. To kalon, to kakon.

The clock-radio is still, la mauvaise foi. What! Is it nothing but that?

Night. The sky is torn and ripped, creating panic in the eye of the beholder. Few look up. The van sits in the duende darkness with the admirable stupidity of officials.

And sleeping beauty Nihilo lies sleeping.

The Bros. depart, the pride of ownership dismantled, pieces to be salvaged in a distant state, checkbook with its pink tongue hanging out.

Sorrow like distant thunder. Brilliant and big on distant O Street the Bros. pass by. O Street that cuts the town in half like a pie, woman sawn in the middle. Middle street of mental merchandise and distant crags.

Sun goes to the end of the road with immense self-pity. Rises the same on the opposite side, catatonic in beauty, showered with glory and dimes.

Love is the exact reverse of desire. O. In the act of love the person goes out of himself. O. It goes forth toward the object; it is continuous; it is fluid. O.

Delacroix: I write to Mlle. de Forget.

Daughter: Kitty, you bust my masterpiece!

from The Place of Love

Bath-Sheba

And I will yet be more vile than thus, and will be base in mine own sight: and of the maidservants which thou hast spoken of, of them shall I be had in honor.

I

And it came to pass in the evening
When the heat melts in the sky like lead
And the breeze comes from Baal-Hamon,
King David rose from his purple bed
And walked upon the house-top with a kingly tread.

Into the markets of the town
Into the streets and gateways he looked down
Serene and comely as the evening star,
And there beheld beside a garden path
A woman bending at her bath.

The King gazed, gazed as the sun
On a distant flower, imparting fire.
He touched his messenger and said,
"Bring this woman to my bedstead."
The servant turned and raised his head:
"Lord, shall I to your chamber bring
The wife of the King's man, Uriah,
The wife of a soldier of the King?"

David leaned on the heavy parapet
And spoke not another word.
Ruddy and beautiful is the Lord's man
And a prince's silence can be heard.

2

With wanton eyes Bath-Sheba
That was faithful in her constancy
Lies on the couch of Judah
And luxuriates in adultery.
With nose-rings and silken veils,
Headbands and earrings and tiaras,
With jewellery on her thighs,
Linen and crisping pins,
Tinkle of gold and silver,
Bath-Sheba laughs and sins.
Her girdle too is spicy,
The kiss between her breasts
Henna-flower and hyacinth.
Honey is her nether lip.

He with his cunning harp
And golden hands that slew the bear
Applies his love and beauty,
Binds and unbinds her hair.
The kiss of David savors
Sweetly of myrrh and holiness;
Before their God the lovers
Dress and undress and dress.

The Ark and the Law are embattled
But War and Time are both beguiled;
She sends to say in a letter,
"My Lord, I am with child."

3

At length Uriah by King David brought
To the royal chair, stands and looks pale
And speaks as one from battle, angry and hot,
Newly released; his thumbs upon his belt
And fingering the proud and studded hilt.
Impatiently he turns and speaks in brief
Of archers fallen, chariots overturned,
Ram-battered towers, and much of running blood,
Friends struck and armor ignominiously
Melted in fire, claimed and fought upon.
To whom the King, quiet and slow of speech,
"Go to thy house and wife; great is your tale,
Great is your journey and your works of blood;
Rest before fighting. Go into thy house."
And now the soldier, white with rage, "O King,
Still in thy tents, the Ark and Israel,
Judah and all abide, and on thy fields
All sway the doubtful outcome of thy God.
For yet the servants of the Almighty stand
Under His captaincy and thine to rule:
Shall I then go into my house and drink,
Lie with my wife and kiss and sleep at noon
But to be taken like a girl alive
Screaming for life and virtue? Now, by my soul
I swear to join my fellows to their last
And fall upon no couches in my death!"

4

King David sealed a letter
And sent it by Uriah's hand
To the chieftain of his armies
That fought to save the Promised Land.

The chieftain read in the letter
That Uriah should wield his sword
In the thick of the hottest battle,
Where he should die for his Lord.

The chieftain wrote to King David
Who lay with Bath-Sheba in a purple bed,
"Abimilech is slain by a woman
And thy servant Uriah also is dead."
King David wrote to his chieftain,
"We fight at the word of Abraham's Lord;
Be courageous and turn the battle
For many and many shall fall by your sword."

But the woman heavily mourned
And wept for Uriah dead.
Not even for the kisses and the words of David
Would she arise and be comforted,
Until King David asked her to wed
And come as a bride to his purple bed,—
And the mourning and the marriage were scarcely done
Before Bath-Sheba bore the King a son.

5

But Jehovah turned upon his servant David
And struck his child so that it lay
Daily and nightly between life and death,
And David rent his clothes and came to pray.

David lay down on the cold earth.

David ate no food and spoke no word.

David lay for seven days and scarcely stirred.

And on the seventh day the servants came and said,

"Lord David, Lord David, the child is dead."
And they feared his grief.

But the King turned from his tears and rose
And washed and anointed his head
And put on spices and majestic clothes
And worshipped the Lord and ate his bread,
And all the people marvelled, but King David said,

"While the child still breathed
I wept and fasted,
For the weight of prayer
Is as gold and fair
In the sight of the Lord;
And my grief has lasted
For seven days
And now the scales are made to yield
And doubt is dead and grief is healed,
I give the Lord praise.
Lay the child upon the sod;
I have felt the hand of God."

And the Lord blessed David with another son,
The greatest of the monarchs, King Solomon.
He wore purple linen; he wore golden shoes;
He was King of the poets, and he ruled the Jews;
He was honored by the nations, the dead and alive;
His songs were a thousand and a thousand and five;
He had a thousand women in a single room;
He built a palace a temple and a golden tomb.
Bath-Sheba was his mother, beautiful to see,
And she lay with King David in adultery.

New and Uncollected Poems

The Bathers

Man and woman, they enter the sea,
The animal-blue, the bovine slippery wave
That, rising, bares its corrugations
And, falling, takes them in its silky teeth
Tightly, while the vast body mills around
Their already watery bodies, till, half blind,
They pass invisibly through its bony sheath,
Swallowed alive and gasping and let go.

They do not even hear the crash of it
Behind them, where it wrecks itself on land,
But are already willed by water,
Weightless and far gone in forgetfulness.

And they are born in that unrisen sky
Out there where all is bright and water-galled
And the loose guts of water tangle them
And then dissolve; where only the dead wave
Comes back awhile, dissipated
And scattered on the wide wash of the sea.

The bathers, blissful in primeval tears,
Forgotten even by the sea itself
That rocks them absently, two bobbing heads,
Onions or oranges
Dumped by the freight of summer on the sea.

They lose even the power of speech;
They must go back to learn;
They make the difficult return
Where nets of water hold them, feel their legs,
Cast ropes of coldness round their bellies,
Trip them, throw gravel at their ankles,
Until, unpredictably, the entire sea
Makes them a path and gives them a push to the beach.

And they lie down between the yellow boats
Where the sun comes and picks them out
And rubs its fire into their sea-pale flesh,
Rubbing their blood, licking their heavy hair,
Breathing upon their words with drying fire.

New Museum

Entering the new museum we feel first
The rubbery values of a doctor's walls,
Cinnamon, buff, gunmetal, rose of gray,
But these almost immediately fade away,
Leaving the windowless white light
That settles only on the works of art—
A far cry from the stained cathedrals where
Masterpieces crack in the bad air
Of candle grease, conversation, and prayer
Ours is the perfect viewing atmosphere.

Walking around, we are much quieter here
Than in the great basilicas,
The great basilicas of Christendom.
Those freezing niches were the masters' home;
Our galleries warm us like a hotel room
Of cinnamon, powder blue, eggshell of rose,
And yet our painters paint as from a bruise,
The blues neither transparent nor opaque,
The blacks so dry they seem a dust of black.
These are the patterns which our feelings make.

They paint their images as if through smoke,
With now and then a falling coal of red
And now and then a yellow burst, like shock;
They paint the damaged tissue magnified,
The lower land, the structure of the thing;
They paint the darkened luminous optic lake
Through which our eyes, though blind,
See all the lines of force and points of stress
In the scientific field of dark.
These are the patterns which our feelings make.

There is such light in darkness that we see
Blueprints of dreams, child's play, prehistory,
And caves and Altamiras of the mind;
These painters kiss with open eyes to make
Miles of Picassos and the double nose.
Soothed by the blues and blacks, our eyes unclose
To drink great gulps of darkness in;
O skies that fall away time after time
Where tracers of emotion miss the mark
But leave the patterns which our feelings make!

These images have all come home like crows
That cross the hot wheat of the last van Goghs
And cross everything out;
His sorrow saw the thick-skinned peeling sun
Explode above the terrified sunflowers.
Our painters stumble through his private night,
Follow the weak shout of the electric light
Deeper into the caves and offices
Where doctors hang abstractions, blue and black.
These are the patterns which our feelings make.

Manhole Covers

The beauty of manhole covers—what of that?
Like medals struck by a great savage khan,
Like Mayan calendar stones, unliftable, indecipherable,
Not like the old electrum, chased and scored,
Mottoed and sculptured to a turn,
But notched and whelked and pocked and smashed
With the great company names
(Gentle Bethlehem, smiling United States).
This rustproof artifact of my street,
Long after roads are melted away will lie
Sidewise in the grave of the iron-old world,
Bitten at the edges,
Strong with its cryptic American,
Its dated beauty.

Cadillac

Your luna moths bring poems to my eyes,
Your oriflamme brings banners to my slums;
You are fat and beautiful, rich and ugly,
A boiler with gold leaf floral decorations;
You are a hard plush chair with sloping shoulders
In which Victoria, like a kangaroo,
Raises her blazing arms to a poem by Mr. Tennyson.

In the sewing machine of your mind you mend my flags,
Under your forehead fatted sheep are feeding,
Falcons are climbing at unwritten speeds,
Adding machines are singing your arias,
Your motor playing chess with continents,
With Quincy, Illinois, with Hell, New Jersey,
Halting on Oriental rugs in Fez.
Beautiful are your fine cartouches,
Your organ pipes externalized like tusks.

If only I could put my arm around you,
If only I could look you in the eye,
I would tell you a grave joke about turtles' eggs,
But there are always your ostrich plumes,
The hydrangeas drooping between your breasts.
I am afraid of your prosthetic wrists,
The mason jars of your white corpuscles.

For Christmas I will send you Maeterlinck's *Life of the Bee*.

Priests are praying for your beautiful passengers;
Sacraments are burning in your barley-sugar lighthouses;
You carry wild lawyers over yellow bridges;
Your soul as slow as honey coils in vats.

Voluptuous feather-plated Pegasus,
You carry the horizontal thoughtful dead
To golf greens and to sculpture yards of peace.
On leafy springs, O Love, O Death,
Your footfall is the silence that perfects.

I see you everywhere except in dreams.

Western Town

Strange western town at the round edge of night,
Into your sleep the broad-shouldered train
Gentles its way, absorbed in its thundrous quiet,
Shearing off porches of carpenter's gothic,
Gathering bulbs and crocuses of electricity.
Now the green blinds of country stores go down
And arches of gold lettering gleam
Like old asbestos in dead movie houses.

Heart-heavy in the cool compartments
The traveling men turn over in their sleep
As the pale squares of light, newspaper thin,
Fall on their eyelids again and again and again,
Plunging the sleepers into a deeper sleep,
A deeper drift of linen than their dream.

Perhaps a single figure is let down
In the hometown dark, or maybe not;
Perhaps only the sleepy sacks of mail
Or a lone coffin come by rail
At rest now on a sketchy cart. Tomorrow,
Somewhere the city will take the train apart.

Party in Winter

Through jaggedy cliffs of snow, along sidewalks of glass,
Footing unsure, as on a fun-house floor,
A little girl goes, all dressed in black, a Prince
Hamlet himself. In black velvet dress
(under her coat), black stockings (really tights)
And patent leather pumps, solemn white face,
And finally white frill blouse and a gold locket
As a finishing touch, she makes her way,
Bearing an enormous pink and tinfoil box
Tied with a bow of deeper pink.

The box reflects its blush along the high snow walls
As the little prince slips hurriedly up the path
And turns three doors away like a live toy
Into the castle of the birthday party.

Calling the Child

From the third floor I beckon to the child
Flying over the grass. As if by chance
My signal catches her and stops her dance
Under the lilac tree;
And I have flung my net at something wild
And brought it down in all its loveliness.
She lifts her eyes to mine reluctantly,
Measuring in my look our twin distress.

Then from the garden she considers me
And, gathering joy, breaks from the closing net
And races off like one who would forget
That there are nets and snares.
But she returns and stands beneath the tree
With great solemnity, with legs apart,
And wags her head at last and makes a start
And starts her humorous marching up the stairs.

A Garden in Chicago

In the mid-city, under an oiled sky,
I lay in a garden of such dusky green
It seemed the dregs of the imagination.
Hedged round by elegant spears of iron fence
My face became a moon to absent suns.
A low heat beat upon my reading face;
There rose no roses in that gritty place
But blue-gray lilacs hung their tassels out.
Hard zinnias and ugly marigolds
And one sweet statue of a child stood by.

A gutter of poetry flowed outside the yard,
Making me think I was a bird of prose;
For overhead, bagged in a golden cloud,
There hung the fatted souls of animals,
While at my eyes bright dots of butterflies
Turned off and on like distant neon signs.

Assuming that this garden still exists,
One ancient lady patrols the zinnias
(She looks like George Washington crossing the Delaware),
The janitor wanders to the iron rail,
The traffic mounts bombastically out there,
And across the street in a pitch-black bar
With midnight mirrors, the professional
Takes her first whiskey of the afternoon—

Ah! It is like a breath of country air.

Lines for a Unitarian Church

Little church of simple steel I-beams
Set among the squat midwestern houses,
You seem to say and I believe
Body and soul are one,
Man for the world and the world only,
For there is no evil.

Little church without a steeple,
Without the cross, the sword-hilt in the sky,
Without the crazed-glass staining the mystic floor,
You seem to say and I believe
Evil does not exist.

Church of laughter, church of light,
No more the gothic hell, psychotic tower,
Barb-wire star, cruel crescent, mandala,
No more the brothel of the nave, chancre of Guilt
In God's love-nest.

Instead, upon your lawn at church o'clock
A native head sunk in the earth,
A native head chin-deep in the land;
Here the eternal native welcomes you
Welcomes your earliest and best nature,
Welcomes the resurrection into touch.

Little church of friendly steel,
No higher than a human house, as strong,
Beautiful in humid Cincinnati,
Beautiful in the world, inside and out.

The House

We walked over here when it was summer field
And every tree for acres had been felled.
A tumbleweed, the roundness of the world.
Steered close to us and ferried up the hill.
We walked to the dark sill of the excavation
And crossed elastic planks above the pit;
There was impressionable paving, open pipe.
We passed within the cage of wooden ribs,
Gleaming with nails all pointing straight at us.
We ducked through vines of poison-colored wires,
Past the bathtub like a sarcophagus
Crated. Masons were clinking spotless bricks
Pragmatically. We opened the first door,
As a man opens a safe deposit box.
We walked on sod covering the earthen wound;
Squares of live rug gave underfoot like flesh.
Keys were mated with reluctant locks.
Current set up its brilliant nervous system.
We walked on wisps of blond excelsior
And read crimped headlines out of packing cases.
We caught three mice in the acoustical tile;
Three little backs were broken on quick springs.
We sawed and tacked and swept and kissed and cursed
And laid in books and wood and bought a set
Of aluminum numbers and shaved the gray new glass
With razor blades. We slept in whited smells,
Undressed uncurtained in a treeless world.

The Poetry Reading

He takes the lectern in his hands
And, like a pilot at his instruments,
Checks the position of his books, the time,
The glass of water, and the slant of light;
Then, leaning forward on guy-wire nerves,
He elevates the angle of his nose
And powers his soul into the evening.

Now, if ever, he must begin to climb
To that established height
Where one hypnotically remains aloft,
But at the thought, as if an engine coughed,
He drops, barely clearing the first three rows,
Then quakes, recovers, and upward swerves,
And hangs there on his perilous turning fans.

O for more altitude, to spin a cloud
Of crystals, as the cloud writes poetry
In nature's wintry sport!
Or for that hundred-engined voice of wings
That, rising with a turtle in its claws,
Speeds to a rock and drops it heavily,
Where it bursts open with a loud report!

O for that parchment voice of wrinkled vowels,
That voice of all the ages, polyglot,
Sailing death's boat
Past fallen towers of foreign tours—
The shrouded voice troubled with stony texts,
Voice of all souls and of sacred owls,
Darkly intoning from the tailored coat!

Or for the voice of order, witty and good,
Civilizing the ears of the young and rude,
Weaving the music of ideas and forms,
Writing encyclopedias of hope.
Or for that ever higher voice that swarms
Like a bright monkey up religion's rope
To all those vacant thrones.

But he who reads thinks as he drones his song:
What do they think, those furrows of faces,
Of a poet of the middle classes?
Is he a poet at all? His face is fat.
Can the anthologies have his birthday wrong?
He looks more like an aging bureaucrat
Or a haberdasher than a poet of eminence.

He looks more like a Poet-in-Residence

O to be *declassé*, or low, or high,
Criminal, bastard, or aristocrat—
Anything but the norm, the in-between!
Oh, martyr him for his particular vice,
Make him conspicuous at any price,
Save him, O God, from being nice.

Whom the gods love die young. Too late for that,
Too late also to find a different job,
He is condemned to fly from room to room
And, like a parakeet, be beautiful,
Or, like a grasshopper in a grammar school,
Leap for the window that he'll never find,
And take off with a throb and come down blind.

Photographs of the Poets On Looking into a Recent Anthology

As if the inner voice had said, *Don't smile*,
Not one is smiling, as photographers prefer,
But each poet has his chin up, so to speak,
And each poet is in profile, as it were.
The compositions on the whole are weak
And yet suggest the formal Brady style.

Poets are good-looking. It's hard to say just why.
The mouths are poor, often the lips are fat,
The hair of an obvious or a dated cut.
It's difficult to point to this or that
Feature—the ears, for instance—and say what
Precisely makes the pictures catch the eye.

In little ovals and cropped squares they pose,
The sensual, the ethereal, and the vain,
And jut their graceful jawbones into view.
Sometimes the cheeks show deeper grooves of pain
Than in most faces. Nevertheless it's true
The really telltale organ is the nose.

The poet's nose is like a bird in flight;
The winged nostrils buff the shining wind.
The poet's nose is like a speeding prow
That splits the silk of waves and leaves behind
The widening incision of the bow;
The poet's nose is like a bull-tongue plow.

But lesser men have noble noses, too.
It is the look that makes the poet's face;
The look of inside-out, the look of wax,
Of wizened innocence and the skinless gaze;
It is the staring mask that never cracks
Or, when it does, splits dangerously through.

Aged and beardless boys with doubled fists
And girls, old girls, in sibylline disguise,
What is it that the popping camera asks
The flickering silence of your rows of eyes?
What light can penetrate your ancient masks
Or the bright glow of your myopic mists?

Tornado Warning

It is a beauteous morning but the air turns sick,
The April freshness seems to rot, a curious smell.
Above the wool-pack clouds a rumor stains the sky,
A fallow color deadening atmosphere and mind.
The air gasps horribly for breath, sucking itself
In spasms of sharp pain, light drifts away.
Women walk on grass, a few husbands come home,
Bushes and trees stop dead, children gesticulate,
Radios warn to open windows, tell where to hide.

The pocky cloud mammato-cumulus comes on,
Downward-projecting bosses of brown cloud grow
Lumps on lymphatic sky, blains, tumors, and dugs,
Heavy cloud-boils that writhe in general disease of sky,
While bits of hail clip at the crocuses and clunk
At cars and windowglass.

                        We cannot see the mouth,
We cannot see the mammoth's neck hanging from cloud,
Snout open, lumbering down ancient Nebraska
Where dinosaur lay down in deeps of clay and died,
And towering elephant fell and billion buffalo.
We cannot see the horror-movie of the funnel-cloud
Snuffing up cows, crazing the cringing villages,
Exploding homes and barns, bursting the level lakes.

Bad Taste, Inc.

I

There is a shop in Paris called Bad Taste
(Le Mauvais Gout) where objets d'art,
Chiefly Victorian, are sold
To wedding couples from the States,
Interior decorators, movie stars,
Rich poets and other sophisticates.
The past peddles the past
To the latest barbarians. Nothing goes to waste:
Yesterday's newspaper, bits of string,
Forgotten comforts, masterpieces.
In Paris nothing goes to waste,
Especially Taste, especially Bad Taste.

II

In America everything goes to waste.
We waste ourselves in the hygienic sun,
We waste the future, burn it to the ground.
Waste in the States is the national industry,
All are consumers—*consume, consume!*
On to the waste pipe, the cloaca americana!

Human Nature

For months and years in a forgotten war
I rode the battle-gray Diesel-stinking ships
Among the brilliantly advertised Pacific Islands,
Coasting the sinister New Guinea Coasts,
All during the killing and hating of a forgotten war.
Now when I drive behind a Diesel-stinking bus
On the way to the university to teach
Stevens and Pound and Mallarmé,
I am homesick for war.

A Drawerful of Eyeglasses

I have a drawerful of eyeglasses
Which Spinoza or Galileo would have given their eyeteeth
    for:
Green-black prescription glasses,
Glasses for reading or driving,
Even a reading lens for proofreading poems.
What if a tornado ground them up with brick?
What if they were melted by the master-bomb
As the sands of the desert were melted to balls of glass?
What if I couldn't read the latest book
On metaphor or guilt?
What if I had to make up poems in my head
Like Milton or Homer?

Man on Wheels

Cars are wicked, poets think.
Wrong as usual. Cars are part of man.
Cars are biological.
A man without a car is like a clam without a shell.
Granted, machinery is hell,
But carless man is careless and defenseless.
Ford is skin of present animal.
Automobile is shell.
You get yourself a shell or else.

You Call These Poems?

In Hyderabad, city of blinding marble palaces,
White marble university,
A plaything of the Nizam, I read some poetry
By William Carlos Williams, American.
And the educated and the suave Hindus
And the well-dressed Moslems said,
"You call those things poems?
Are those things poems?"

For years I used to write poems myself
That pleased the Moslems and Hindus of culture,
Telling poems in iambic pentameter,
With a masculine inversion in the second foot,
Frozen poems with an ice-pick at the core,
And lots of allusions from other people's books.

Emily Dickinson and Katherine Anne Porter

1

Emily Dickinson's father yanked on the Baptist bell
To call the townspeople to see the sunset,
And the Baptists saw the glory of the sunset
And went home to stained-glass darkness, awfully disap-
    pointed
That something really hideous hadn't happened,
Like Hell or the atom bomb.
Old man Dickinson who also fed the sparrows over the snow
With grain from his barn (age seventy-one)
And hid until he saw them peck it up.

"And drove the fastest horse in town."

2

And when Dylan Thomas was introduced
To Katherine Anne Porter in a room full of people,
He stooped and picked her up below the thighs
And raised her to the ceiling like a drink,
And held her straight in the slack-jawed smoke-blue air
Two minutes, five minutes, seven minutes,
While everybody wondered what it meant
To toast the lady with her own body
Or hold her to the light like a plucked flower.

A Modest Funeral

Death passed by on fervid rubber wheels.
Three broad mortuary Cadillacs,
Flying modest pennants low on the fenders,
Led the procession, followed by a covey
Of medium-priced cars, with no overcrowding,
And some with just a driver at the wheel,
But the whole cluster with headlights lit,
As is the law and custom of the thoroughfare.

Only at the rear was there any sign of jostling,
Any suggestion of impatient thought
At foolish delay, or *Where's the funeral!*

Death passed at moderate speed and slowed the counter-
　　traffic
To a respectful twenty, making it almost veer,
As when one hears a siren in the distance.

Then it was gone, the funeral with its flags
And fine sparkling lights, like tears in the eyes,
Gone to the silvered fences at the edge of town,
And the soft gravel of the cemetery.

Connecticut Valley

Call it the richest pocket of the world,
Which rumored in the ear of Milton's breed
Once bore the freeborn Englishman across,
Or from God-ridden Massachusetts, down.

A while the Indian stinking from his paint
Stalked the white villages and counted scalps
But turned, lacking concealment, to the hills,
Or else fell, richer by a musket ball,

Leaving the land divided, as were fit,
Between the men with implements to scratch,
Rescratch and smooth and currycomb the dirt
March after March unto the present hour.

Good Yankees these, and round about the sane
Practical hearts who fashioned all the nails
For the new nation, carving in spare time
Wooden nutmegs to sell to willing fools;

Ruling themselves by blue laws, painting pure
The plain church, blending beauty with the snow.
Death for adultery in the pretty towns
And strictness in the fields for centuries.

After three hundred years the motorist
Happening by may marvel at these streets
Where every dwelling bears the building date
In homage to the beauty of great age;

Where every ghost is laid, knowing how well
The pride of house is kept, both in the fields
Where dark tobacco sweetens under gauze,
Cows calve, corn stretches to the yellow sun;

And where on lawns the Sunday gentry meet,
Insurance writers, toolmakers in tweeds,
The fibrous sons and daughters of the state
Driving hard bargains through the afternoon.

In India

In India, the people form among the trees
With a rubbery quiet; on farthest roads
Surround you with a rubbery tread.
I stand in their circles of wonder like a light
Shining in eyes grown vague with centuries
Of stunned obedience and heartbreaking loads,
Not tall, I tower above them by a head;
Pale, I pass through their never-ending night.

A crow came to my window by the sea
At four o'clock in the Taj Mahal Hotel;
He cocked his eye and when I turned my back
Flew to my tea tray with a hideous clack
Of beak and claws, turning over the tea
And making off with the cake. The crow did well,
For down below me, where the street was black
With white-clad Hindus, what was there to take?

And foreigners say the poverty is the cause,
Thinking that gold can cure the old disease,
Thinking that oil can make the old wheel turn.
I see a new landmark on the long skyline,
An edifice of seamless stone and glass
Topped by the great word *Standard* in the skies.
Toward the Arabian Sea I watch it burn
And, being American, feel that it is mine!

And still the native voices, soft as sand,
Cry, "Master! Master!" as a professional saint
Might roll his eyes and faint into his god
In the middle of traffic. Still thy call aloud
"Sahib, Master!" and hold out their hand.
And lovely women with a moon of paint
Daubed on their foreheads shake hands and fade
Into silence, bowing with a praying bow.

These beautiful, small millions turn to stone
Before your eyes, become soft sculpture swarming up
The slant of temples, where their thighs protrude
Half out of joint, the angles of their arms
Twist in voluptuous torsion, and their bones
Fold into symbols pliable as rope.
The walls are sluggish with their multitude
Of gods and dancers and half-human forms.

But are they gods or droppings of the gods?
Is this the mire in which they all submerge,
This bog of holiness which ingurgitates
Prophet and hero, turning them to stone?
Which are the deities, which the human clods?
Or in this jungle do they truly merge?
And where is Reason in this hive of faith—
The one god missing from this pantheon?

I see a new god carved in fresh relief,
The brown saint in the shining spectacles
Who took the hand of the untouchables,
Who wove all India from a skein of thread.
Now he and all their spinning wheels are gone,
For a young Hindu, under whose homespun
Lay a revolver, knelt and, in good faith,
Received his blessing and then shot him dead.

California Winter

It is winter in California, and outside
Is like the interior of a florist shop:
A chilled and moisture-laden crop
Of pink camellias lines the path; and what
Rare roses for a banquet or a bride,
So multitudinous that they seem a glut!

A line of snails crosses the golf-green lawn
From the rosebushes to the ivy bed;
An arsenic compound is distributed
For them. The gardener will rake up the shells
And leave in a corner of the patio
The little mound of empty snails, like skulls.

By noon the fog is burnt off by the sun
And the world's immensest sky opens a page
For the exercises of a future age;
Now jet planes draw straight lines, parabolas,
And x's, which the wind, before they're done,
Erases leisurely or pulls to fuzz.

It is winter in the valley of the vine.
The vineyards crucified on stakes suggest
War cemeteries, but the fruit is pressed,
The redwood vats are brimming in the shed,
And on the sidings stand tank cars of wine,
For which bright juice a billion grapes have bled.

And skiers from the snow line driving home
Descend through almond orchards, olive farms,
Fig tree and palm tree—everything that warms
The imagination of the wintertime.
If the walls were older one would think of Rome:
If the land were stonier one would think of Spain.

But this land grows the oldest living things,
Trees that were young when Pharaohs ruled the world,
Trees whose new leaves are only just unfurled.
Beautiful they are not; they oppress the heart
With gigantism and with immortal wings;
And yet one feels the sumptuousness of this dirt.

It is raining in California, a straight rain
Cleaning the heavy oranges on the bough,
Filling the gardens till the gardens flow,
Shining the olives, tiling the gleaming tile,
Waxing the dark camellia leaves more green,
Flooding the daylong valleys like the Nile.

Aubade

What dawn is it?

The morning star stands at the end of your street as you watch me turn to laugh a kind of goodbye, with love-crazed head like a white satyr moving through wet bushes.

The morning star bursts in my eye like a hemorrhage as I enter my car in a dream surrounded by your heavenly-earthly smell.

The steering wheel is sticky with dew,

The golf course is empty, husbands stir in their sleep desiring, and though no cocks crow in suburbia, the birds are making a hell of a racket.

Into the newspaper dawn as sweet as your arms that hold the old new world, dawn of green lights that smear the empty streets with come and go.

It is always dawn when I say goodnight to you,

Dawn of wrecked hair and devastated beds,

Dawn when protective blackness turns to blue and lovers drive sunward with peripheral vision.

To improvise a little on Villon

Dawn is the end for which we are together.

My house of loaded ashtrays and unwashed glasses, tulip petals and columbine that spill on the table and splash on the floor,

My house full of your dawns,

My house where your absence is presence,

My slum that loves you, my bedroom of dustmice and cobwebs, of local paintings and eclectic posters, my bedroom of rust neckties and divorced mattresses, and of two of your postcards, *Pierrot with Flowers* and *Young Girl with Cat*,

My bed where you have thrown your body down like a king's ransom or a boa constrictor.

But I forgot to say: May passed away last night,
May died in her sleep,
That May that blessed and kept our love in fields and
    motels.
I erect a priapic statue to that May for lovers to kiss as long
    as I'm in print, and polish as smooth as the Pope's
    toe.
This morning came June of spirea and platitudes,
This morning came June discreetly dressed in gray,
June of terrific promises and lawsuits.

And where are the poems that got lost in the shuffle of
    spring?
Where is the poem about the eleventh of March, when we
    raised the battleflag of dawn?
Where is the poem about the coral necklace that whipped
    your naked breasts in leaps of love?
The poem concerning the ancient lover we followed through
    your beautiful sleeping head?
The fire-fountain of your earthquake thighs and your electric
    mouth?
Where is the poem about the little one who says my name
    and watches us almost kissing in the sun?
The vellum stretchmarks of your learned belly,
Your rosy-fingered nightgown of nylon and popcorn,
Your razor that caresses your calves like my hands?
Where are the poems that are already obsolete, leaves of
    last month, a very historical month?
Maybe I'll write them, maybe I won't, no matter,
And this is the end for which we are together.
Et c'est la fin pour quoy sommes ensemble.

About the Author

Karl Shapiro

was born in Baltimore, Maryland, and attended the University of Virginia and Johns Hopkins University. In 1946 he was appointed Consultant in Poetry at the Library of Congress, and then, in 1947, he joined the faculty of Johns Hopkins University, where he taught writing courses. From 1950 to 1956 he was editor of Poetry, A Magazine of Verse. *He was professor of English and editor of* The Prairie Schooner *at the University of Nebraska from 1956 to 1966 and professor of English at the Chicago Circle Campus of the University of Illinois from 1966 to 1968. He is now professor of English at the University of California at Davis. He is a member of the National Institute of Arts and Letters. His second volume of verse,* V-Letter and Other Poems, *was awarded the Pulitzer Prize in 1945.*